Primary Skills

Maths 6-7

Sarah Lindsay

This book belongs to:

WHSmith

What your child will learn from this book

This book will help your child cover these areas of maths:

- Reading, writing and counting numbers to 100
- Tens and units
- Adding and taking away to 20
- 2, 5 and 10 times tables
- Odd and even numbers
- Telling the time
- Starting division
- Measuring
- Money
- Fractions

How you can help

A few simple guidelines will ensure that your child gets the best from this book:

- Make sure that you explain what the book is about.

- Do a few examples on a page with your child to ensure she or he understands.

- Encourage your child to do all the exercises on a page but don't expect too much to be done at a time.

- Ensure you understand what your child gets right and wrong. Explain any difficulties and try to provide more practice.

- Give all the praise and encouragement you can.

Page 3 explains how to use this book.

How to use this book

- The book is set out in straightforward two page units. Each unit contains teaching points, exercises and a special challenge:

The Teaching Box
explains new learning simply and directly.

The Exercises
provide lots of practice to ensure the learning is fully understood.

The Challenge Star
at the end of the unit extends your child's skills still further.

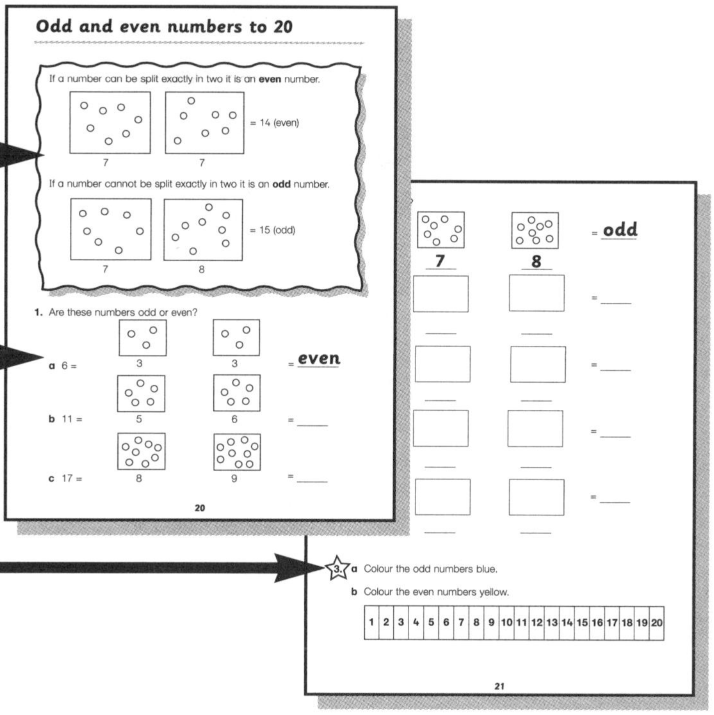

- Throughout the book you will also find regular special checking pages:

Do you remember?
This comes at the front and reminds your child of the basic knowledge needed at the start of the book.

Check-ups
These appear after every few units and give your child a chance to recall what has been covered.

Test yourself
This comes at the end and tests everything covered in the book.

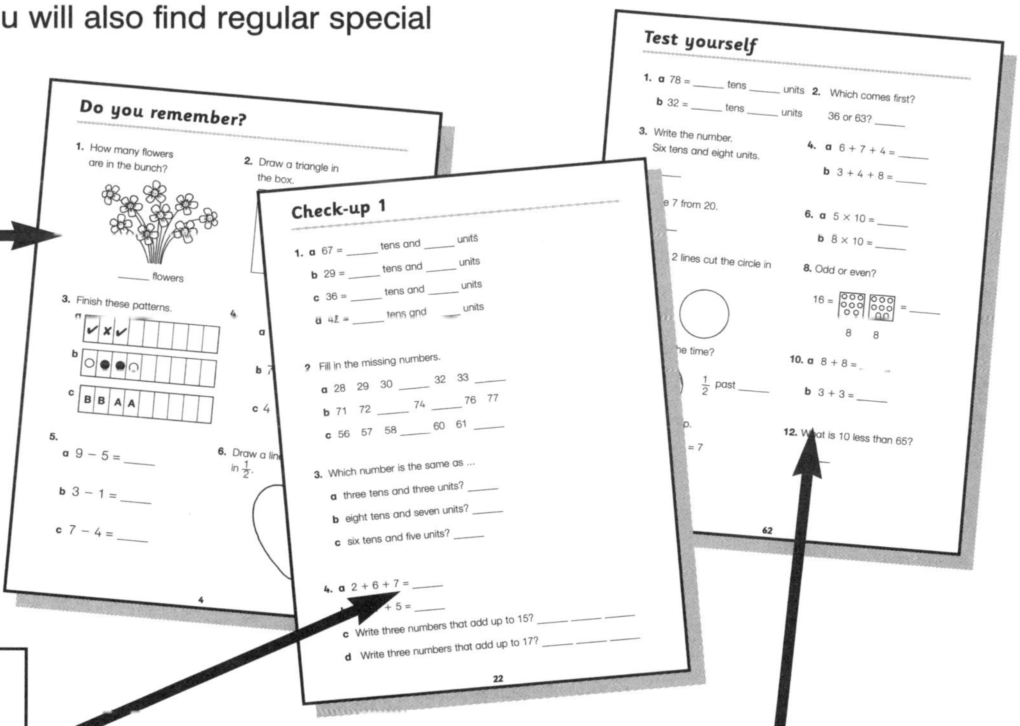

- You will find answers to all the questions in this book at the back.

Do you remember?

1. How many flowers are in the bunch?

______ flowers

2. Draw a triangle in the box.

It has ______ sides.

3. Finish these patterns.

a

✔	✘	✔						

b

○	●	●	○					

c

B	**B**	**A**	**A**					

4.

a $2 + 3 =$ ______

b $7 + 1 =$ ______

c $4 + 4 =$ ______

5.

a $9 - 5 =$ ______

b $3 - 1 =$ ______

c $7 - 4 =$ ______

6. Draw a line to cut this shape in $\frac{1}{2}$.

7. Write in the sign **–** or **+**.

a 8 ______ 3 = 5

b 7 ______ 2 = 9

c 8 ______ 3 = 11

8. Fill in the missing numbers.

a

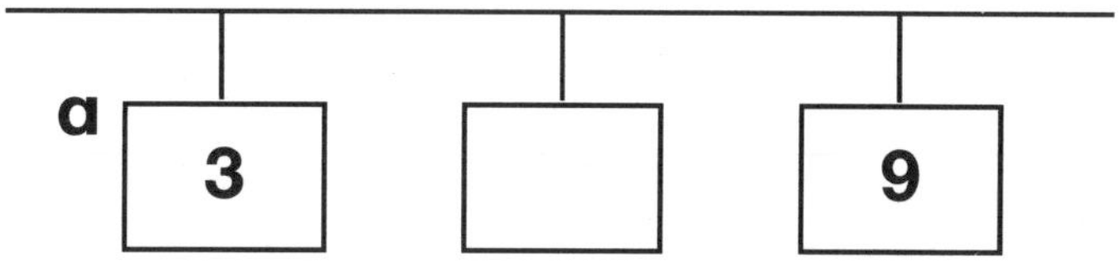

b

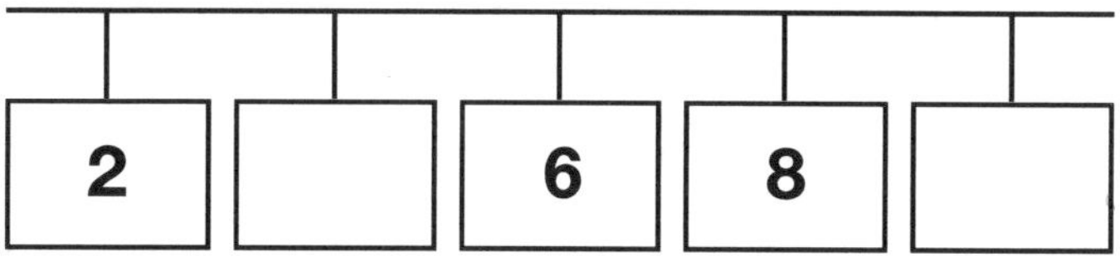

9.

a 16 = 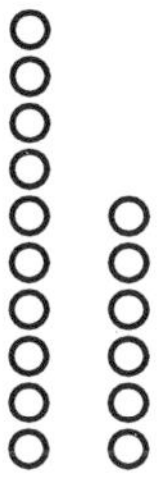 = ______ ten

______ units

b 11 =  = ______ ten

______ unit

10. What is the time?

______ o'clock

11. Colour in the **longer** objects.

or

or

12. Draw two lines to cut the square into $\frac{1}{4}$s.

Read and write numbers to 100

100 = 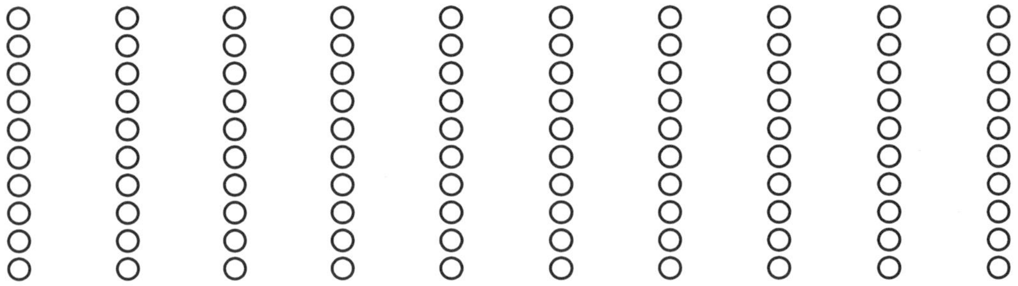

100 = **10 tens**

46 = 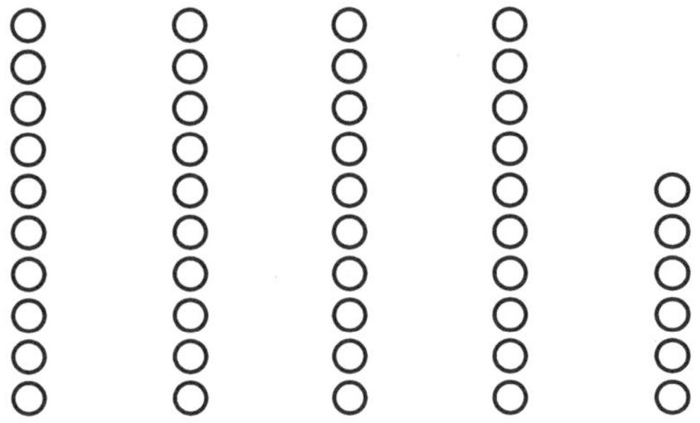

46 = **4 tens 6 units**

1. Colour in the correct number of tens and units. The first one has been done.

a 82 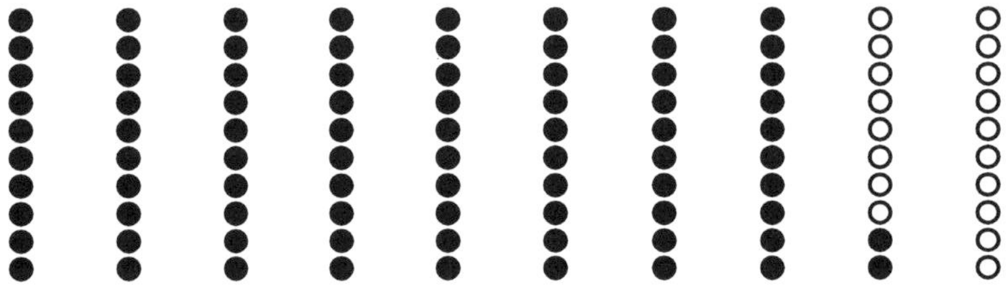

b 64 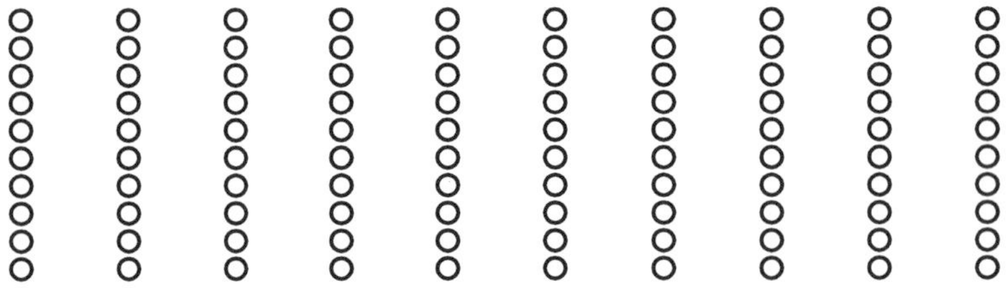

c 35 

2. How many? Write the number.

a 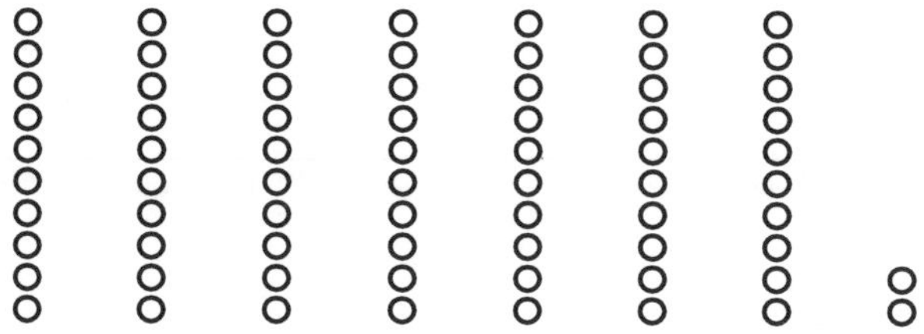 = ______

b 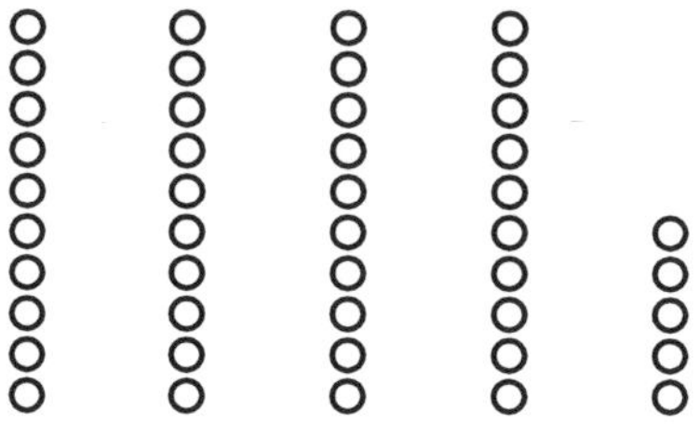 = ______

c 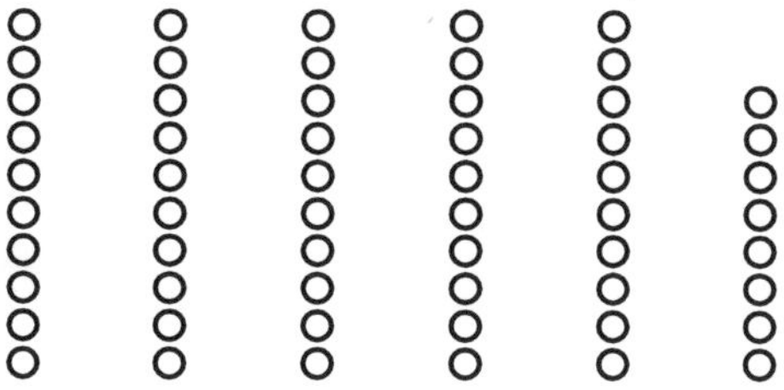 = ______

3. **a** 53 = ______ tens ______ units **b** 28 = ______ tens ______ units

c 97 = ______ tens ______ units **d** 36 = ______ tens ______ units

4. Circle the number shown.

a 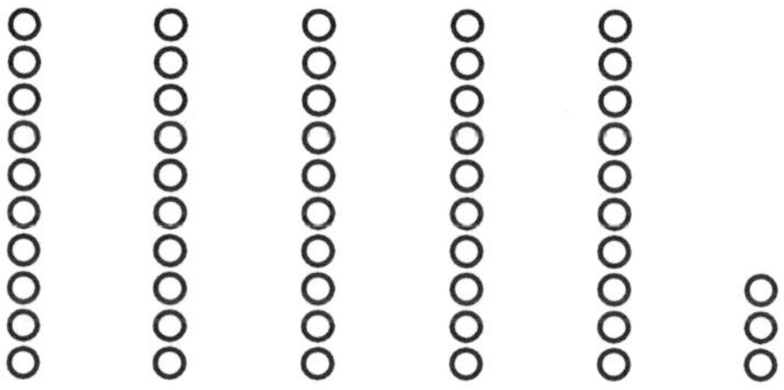 = 68 53 29

b 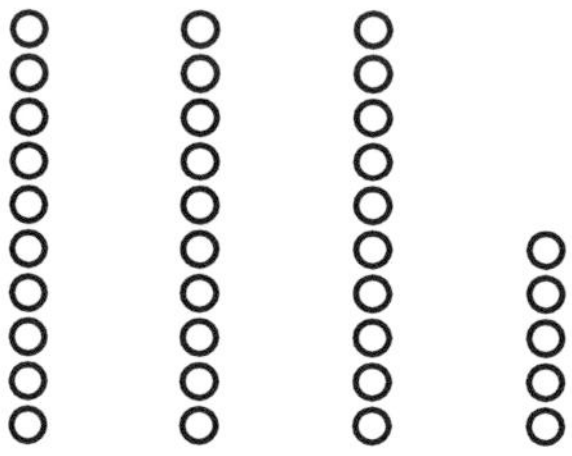 = 35 72 49

c  = 11 21 31

Order and count numbers to 100

Remember, numbers go up in order.

16 17 18 19 **20** 21 22 23 24 25 26 27 28 29 **30** 31

66 67 68 69 **70** 71 72 73 74 75 76 77 78 79 **80** 81

1. Join the dots to make shapes. Start on **x** each time.

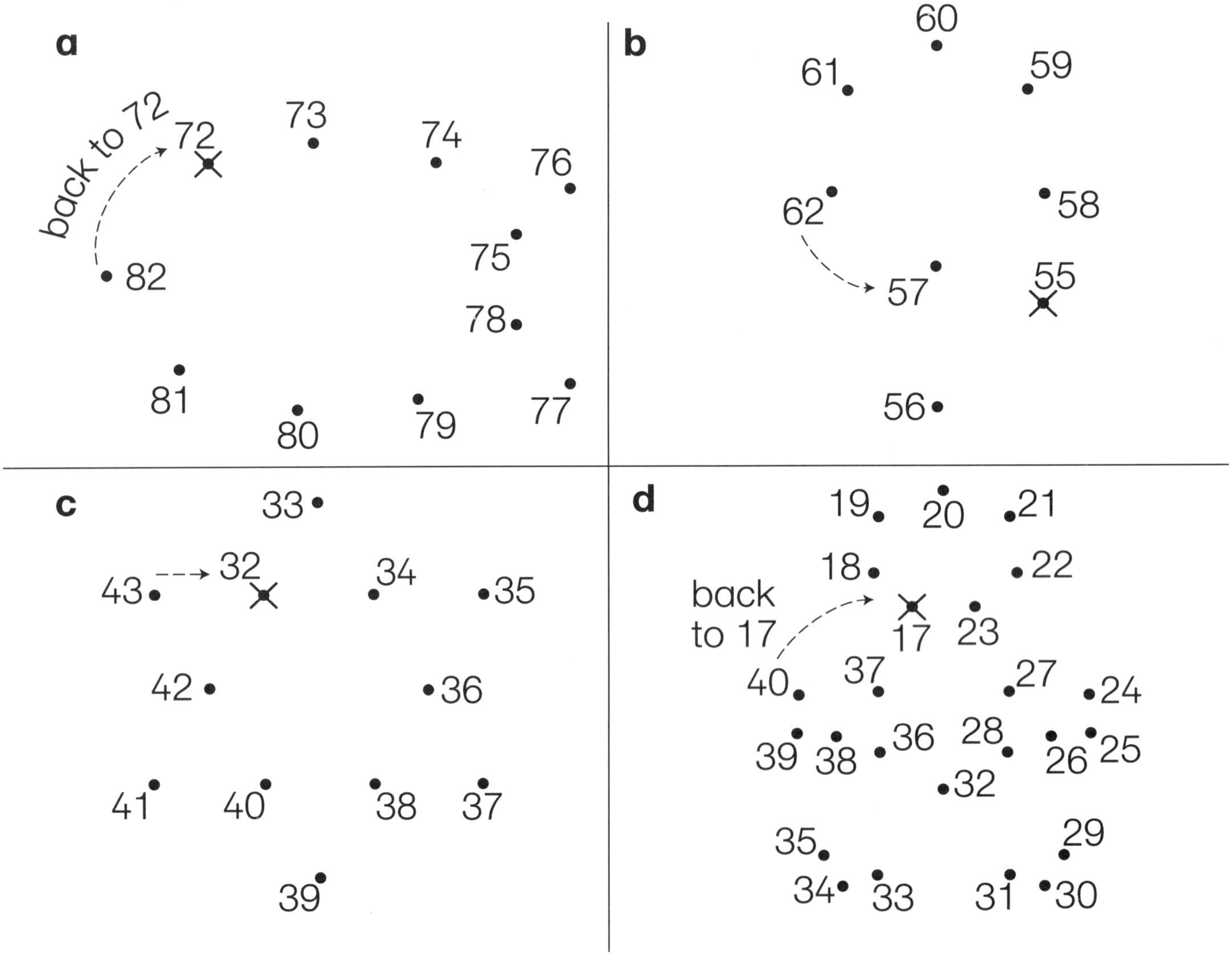

2. Fill in the missing numbers.

a 61 62 63 ______ 65 66

b 47 ______ 49 50 51 52

c 83 84 85 86 ______ 88

d 17 18 ______ 20 ______ 22

e 26 27 28 ______ 30 ______

3. Which number is smaller?

a 68 or 45? ______

b 21 or 33? ______

c 83 or 73? ______

d 12 or 11? ______

e 38 or 29? ______

f 46 or 64? ______

g 28 or 18? ______

h 22 or 12? ______

i 57 or 55? ______

j 69 or 77? ______

k 32 or 17? ______

l 51 or 55? ______

4. Write a number that comes between the two numbers.

a 21 24 26

b 38 ______ 41

c 19 ______ 24

d 29 ______ 33

e 31 ______ 33

f 68 ______ 72

g 97 ______ 99

h 68 ______ 73

Tens and units

Look at the number 43.

43 is 4 tens and 3 units.

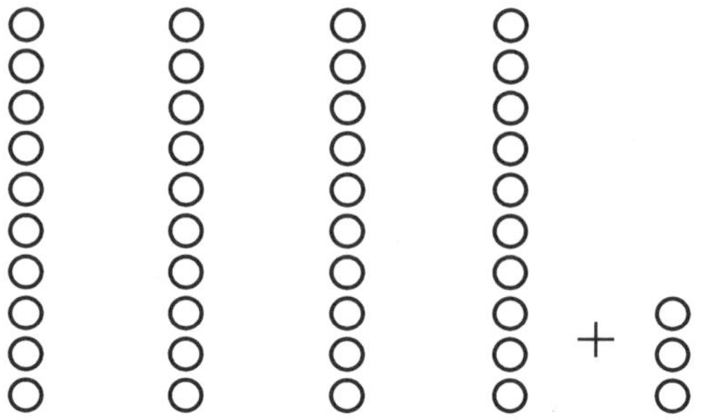

1. Fill in the gaps.

a 63 = 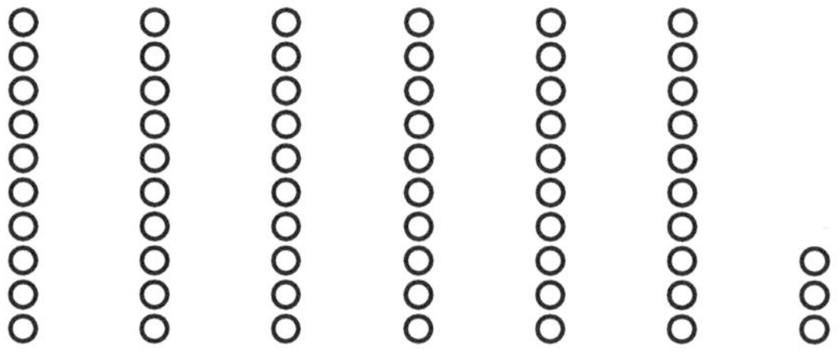 = ______ tens ______ units

b 28 =  = ______ tens ______ units

c 35 = 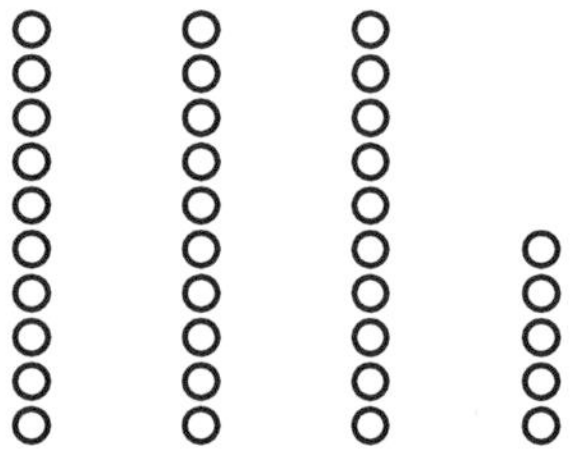 = ______ tens ______ units

d 76 =  = ______ tens ______ units

2. How many tens and units?

a 23 = **2** tens and **3** units

b 48 = ______ tens and ______ units

c 57 = ______ tens and ______ units

d 89 = ______ tens and ______ units

e 62 = ______ tens and ______ units

f 99 = ______ tens and ______ units

g 73 = ______ tens and ______ units

3. Write these numbers in words.

a 47 = **four tens and seven units**

b 29 = ______________________________

c 69 = ______________________________

d 72 = ______________________________

4. Which number is the same as ...

a Six tens and five units? ______

b Nine tens and three units? ______

c Two tens and two units? ______

d Five tens and nine units? ______

Adding more than two numbers

Remember, we can add two numbers.

5 + 2 = 7

1. Add these numbers.

a 7 + 3 = ______ **b** 8 + 4 = ______

c 5 + 6 = ______ **d** 9 + 7 = ______

We can add more than two numbers.

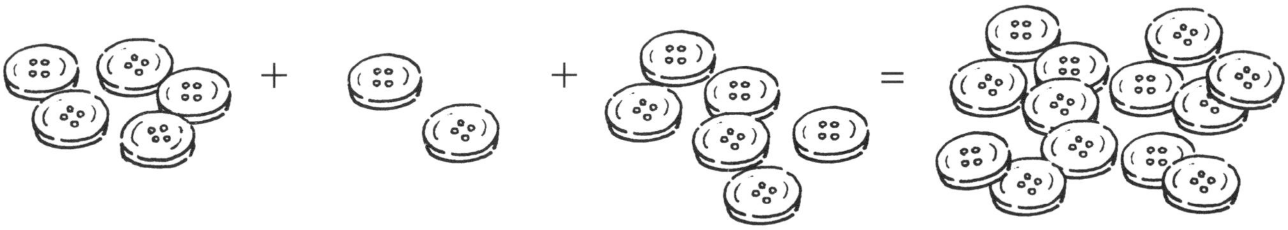

5 + 2 + 6 = 13

2. a Write the missing number. Draw and write the answers.

4 + **3** + **3** =

______ ______ ______ ______

b

______ ______ ______ ______

c

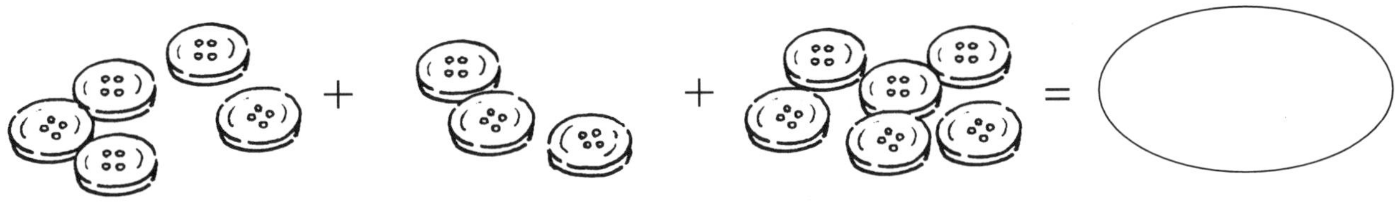

______ ______ ______ ______

3. Add these numbers.

a 6 + 2 + 7 = ______

b 8 + 5 + 6 = ______

c 2 + 9 + 9 = ______

d 10 + 6 + 2 = ______

4. Find the answer.

a Add 5, 2 and 9. ______

b What is the total of 3, 6 and 7? ______

c Write three numbers that add up to 12.

______ ______ ______

d What is the total of 5, 4 and 7? ______

e Write three numbers that add up to 17. ______ ______ ______

Subtraction 1

Do you remember how to subtract?

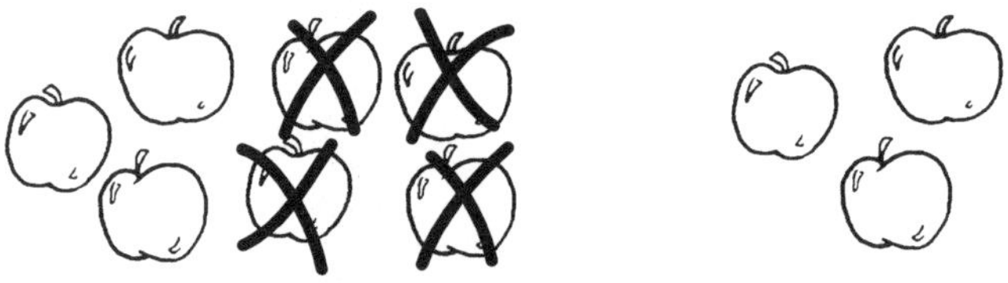

7 – 4 = 3

1. Subtract. Draw the apples. Write the numbers underneath.

a

=

8 – **3** = ______

b

=

______ – ______ = ______

c

=

______ – ______ = ______

2. Now we are going to subtract bigger numbers. Finish these sums.

a

=

13 – **6** = ______

b  = 

______ – ______ = ______

c  =

______ – ______ = ______

d  =

______ – ______ = ______

3. Now try these. Use pictures if it helps.

a 12 – 5 = ______ **b** 17 – 7 = ______

c 20 – 8 = ______ **d** 14 – 7 = ______

4. Find the answers.

a How many less is 7 than 8? ______

b Take 5 from 15. ______

c How many must I take from 20 to leave 12? ______

10 times table

2 lots of 10 is 20

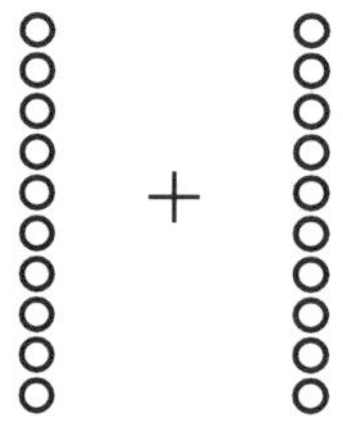

= 20

10 10

2 × 10 = 20

× means 'lots of'

1.

a 5 × 10 =

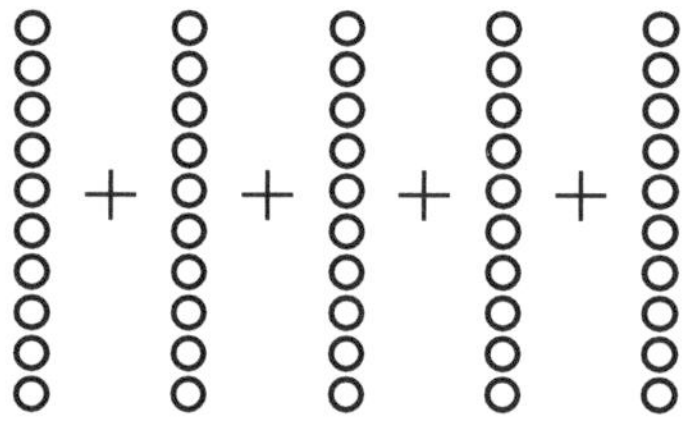

= **50**

b 3 × 10 =

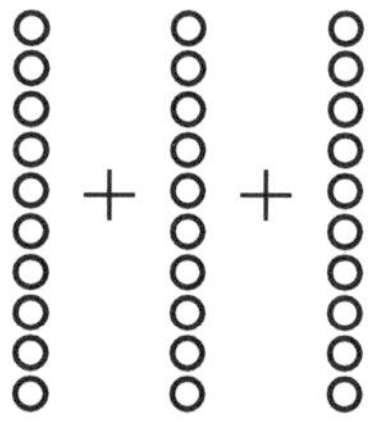

= ______

c 7 × 10 =

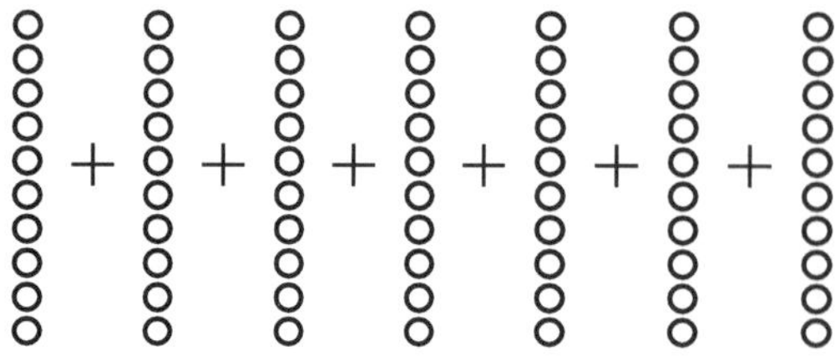

= ______

d 4 × 10 = 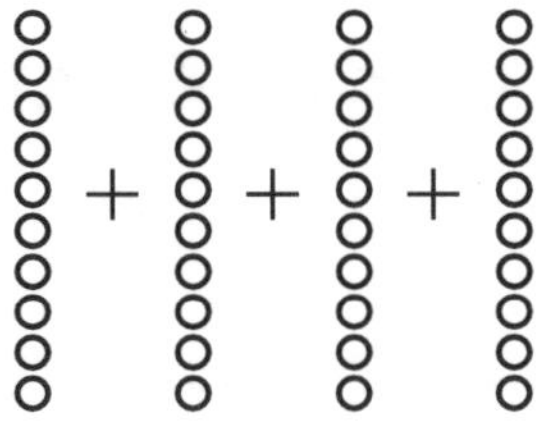 = ______

e 1 × 10 =  = ______

2. 1 × 10 = ______ 6 × 10 = ______

2 × 10 = ______ 7 × 10 = ______

3 × 10 = ______ 8 × 10 = ______

4 × 10 = ______ 9 × 10 = ______

5 × 10 = ______ 10 × 10 = ______

3. Fill in the gaps.

a 6 × 10 = ______ **b** 8 × 10 = ______

c ______ × 10 = 30 **d** ______ × 10 = 50

e 1 × ______ = 10 **f** 2 × ______ = 20

4. Finish these 10 times table lists.

a

10	**20**		**40**		**60**		**80**	

b

10		**30**				**70**	**80**	**90**

Do you remember halves and quarters?

Remember, this is how we cut a cake in half and into quarters.

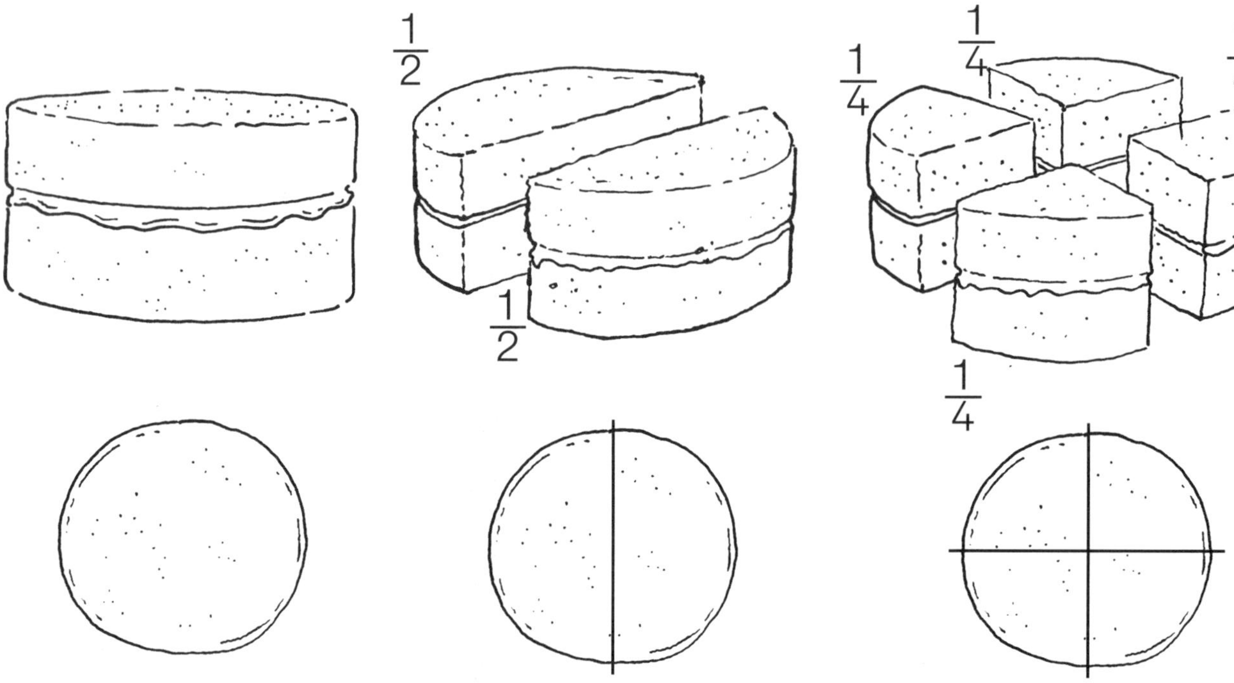

1. Cut these shapes in $\frac{1}{2}$.

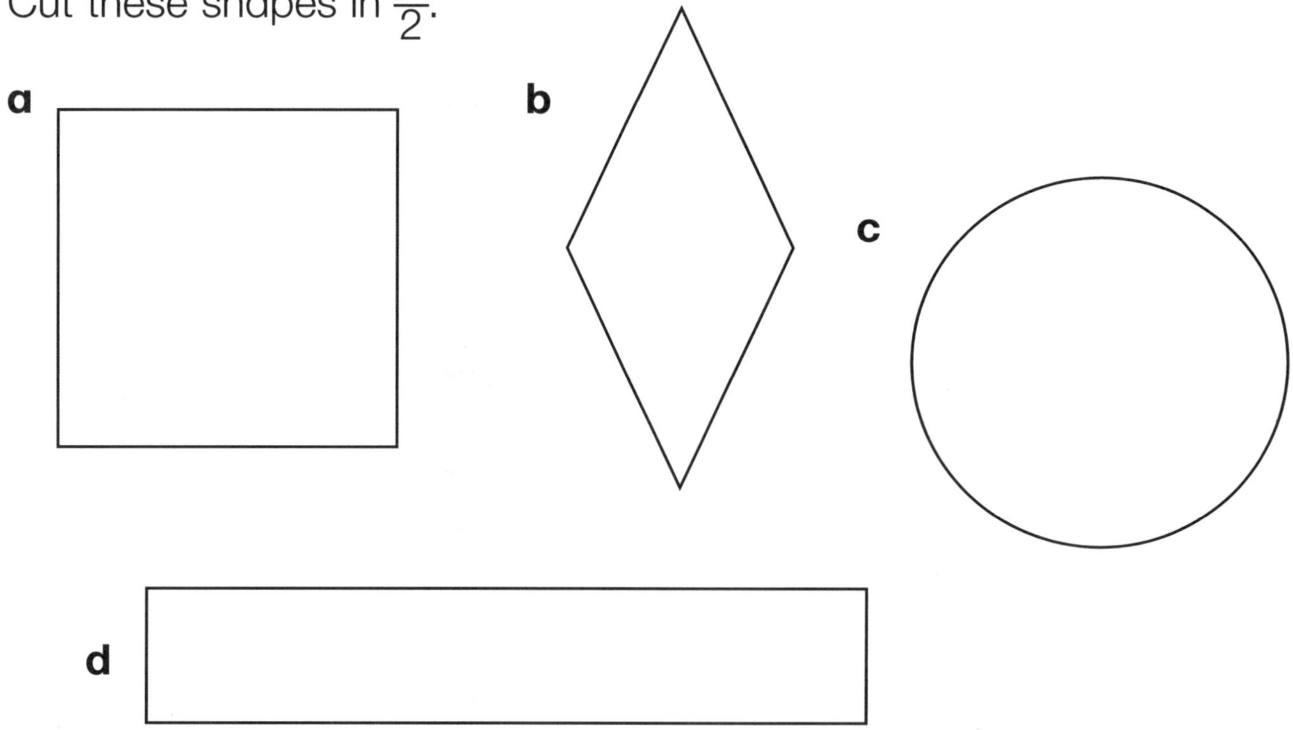

2. Cut these shapes in $\frac{1}{4}$ s.

a

b

c

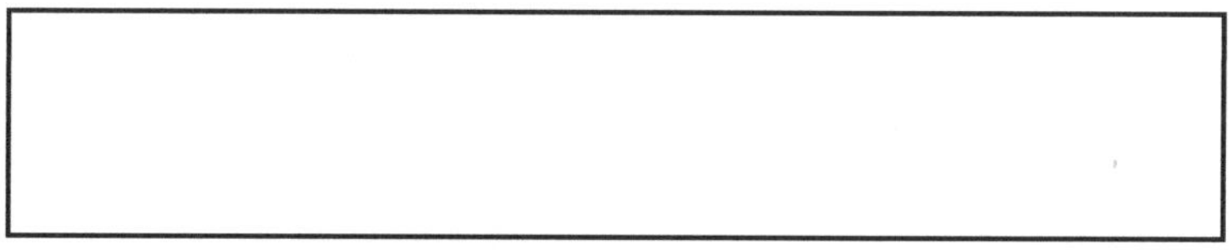

d

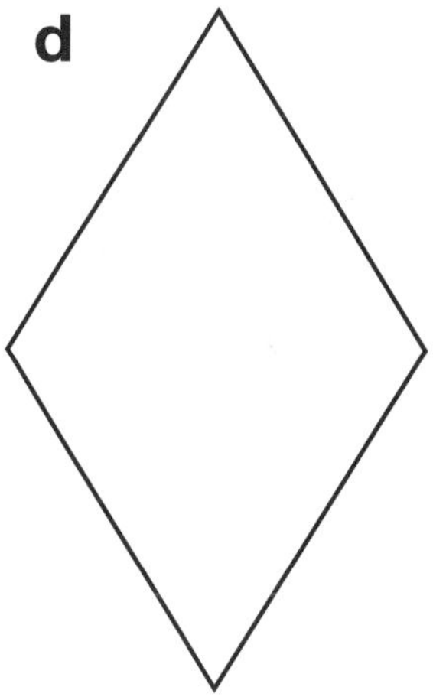

e

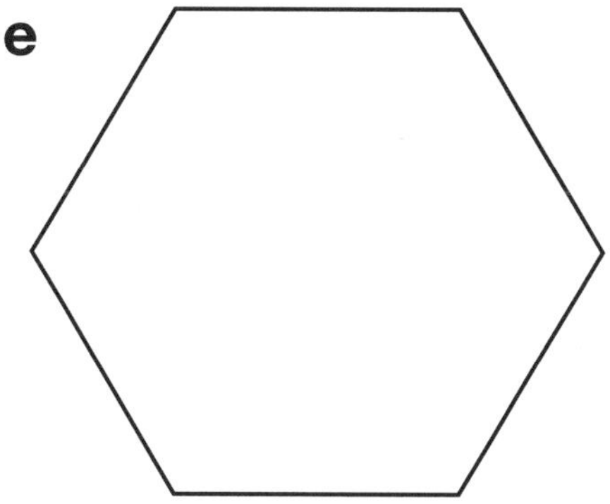

3. Have these objects been cut in $\frac{1}{2}$ s or $\frac{1}{4}$ s?

a

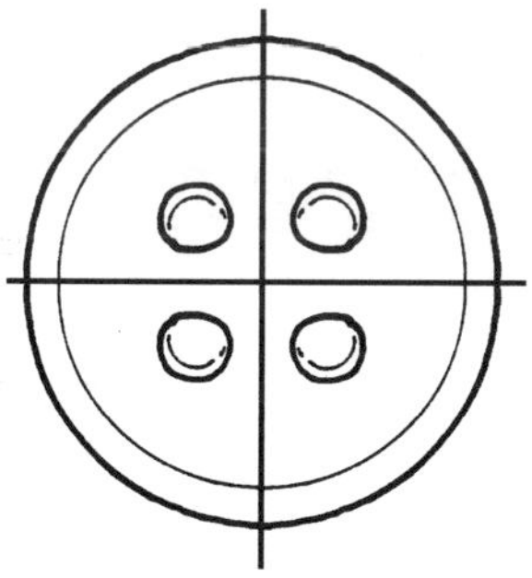

______

b

______

c

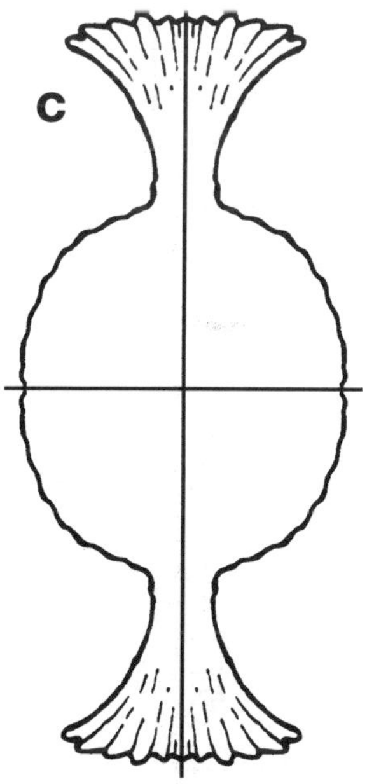

______

d

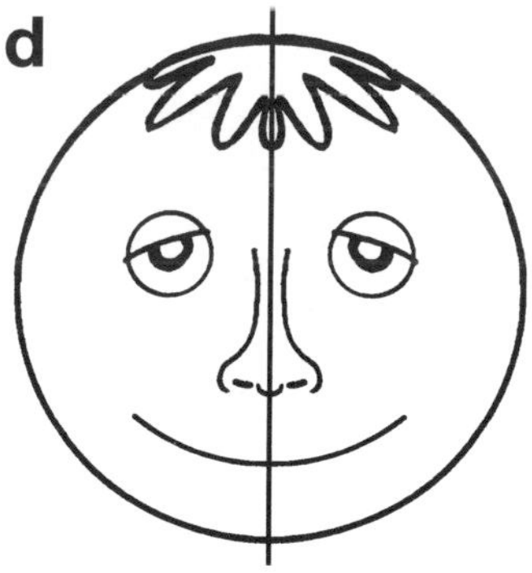

______

Odd and even numbers to 20

If a number can be split exactly in two it is an **even** number.

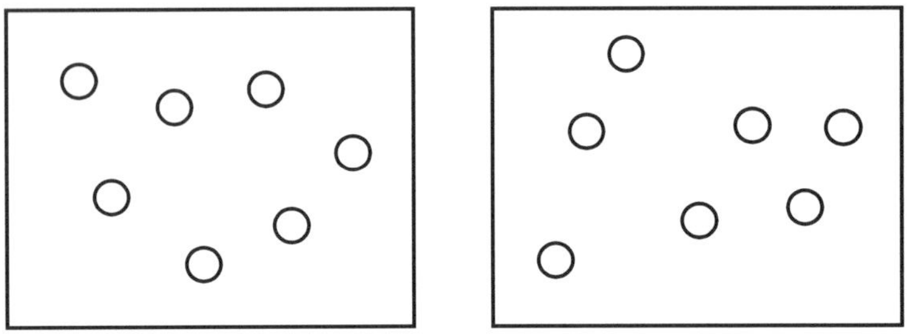

7 7 = 14 (even)

If a number cannot be split exactly in two it is an **odd** number.

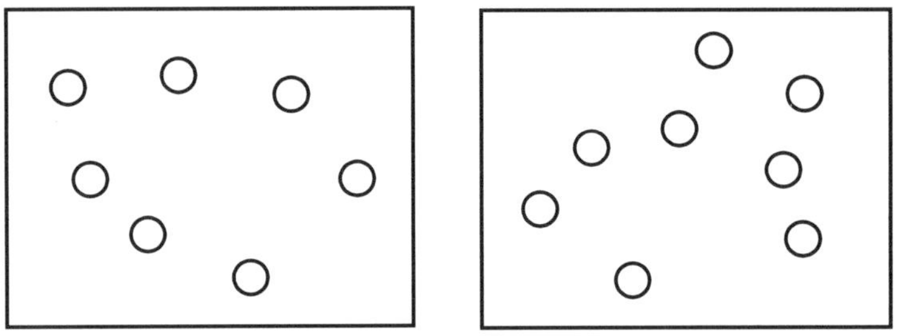

7 8 = 15 (odd)

1. Are these numbers odd or even?

a 6 = 3 3 = even

b 11 = 5 6 = ______

c 17 = 8 9 = ______

2. Odd or even?

a 15 = 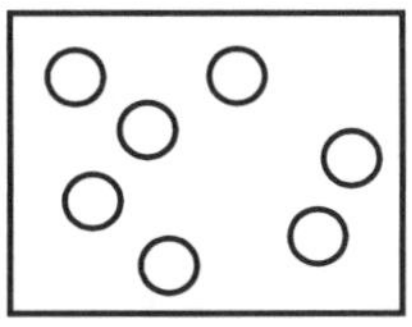 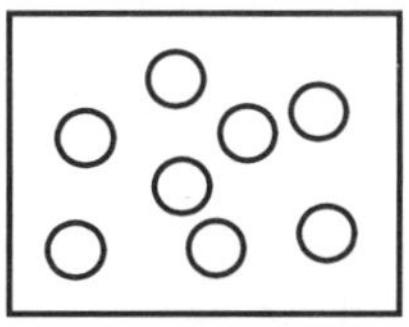 = **odd**

7 **8**

b 8 = ______ ______ = ______

c 19 = ______ ______ = ______

d 13 = ______ ______ = ______

e 18 = ______ ______ = ______

3. **a** Colour the odd numbers blue.

b Colour the even numbers yellow.

1	2	3	4	5	6	7	8	9	10	11	12	13	14	15	16	17	18	19	20

Check-up 1

1. a 67 = ______ tens and ______ units

   b 29 = ______ tens and ______ units

   c 36 = ______ tens and ______ units

   d 42 = ______ tens and ______ units

2. Fill in the missing numbers.

   a 28 29 30 ______ 32 33 ______

   b 71 72 ______ 74 ______ 76 77

   c 56 57 58 ______ 60 61 ______

3. Which number is the same as ...

   a three tens and three units? ______

   b eight tens and seven units? ______

   c six tens and five units? ______

4. a 2 + 6 + 7 = ______

   b 5 + 7 + 5 = ______

   c Write three numbers that add up to 15? ______ ______ ______

   d Write three numbers that add up to 17? ______ ______ ______

5. Do these taking away sums.

a

 −  =

____ − ____ = ____

b

 −  =

____ − ____ = ____

6. **a** $2 \times 10 =$ ____ **b** $7 \times 10 =$ ____

c $3 \times 10 =$ ____ **d** $8 \times 10 =$ ____

7. Cut these shapes in $\frac{1}{4}$ s.

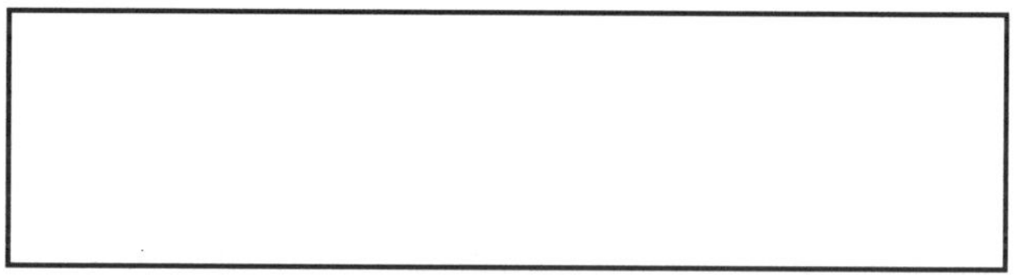

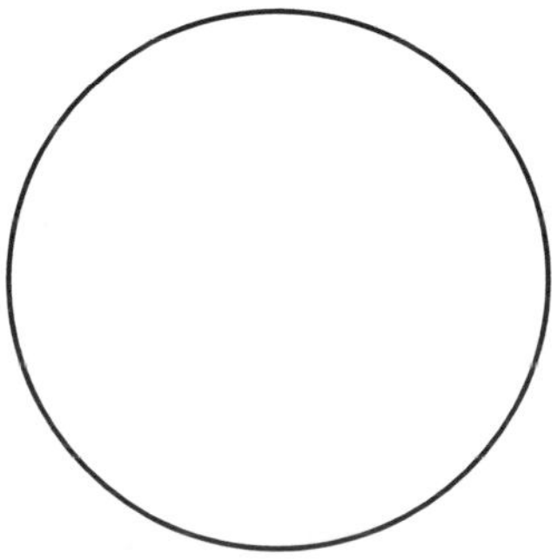

8. Odd or even? Try to split the numbers in half. Write odd or even at the end.

a 16 = = ____

b 13 = = ____

Time – o'clock and half past

This clock shows 5 o'clock.

1. What time do these clocks show?

a

______ o'clock

b

______ o'clock

c

______ o'clock

This clock shows $\frac{1}{2}$ past 5.
When the long hand points at the **6** the time is $\mathbf{\frac{1}{2}}$ **past**.

2. What time do these clocks show?

a

$\frac{1}{2}$ past ______

b

$\frac{1}{2}$ past ______

c

$\frac{1}{2}$ past ______

3. Draw the long hand on these clocks.

a

9 o'clock

b

$\frac{1}{2}$ past 2

c

$\frac{1}{2}$ past 6

d

10 o'clock

e

4 o'clock

f

$\frac{1}{2}$ past 1

4. What time do these clocks show?

a

____

____

b

____

____

5. It is 3 o'clock.

a What will the time be in 1 hour? ______________

b What will the time be in $\frac{1}{2}$ an hour? ______________

c What will the time be in $1\frac{1}{2}$ hours? ______________

Doubling up to 10

Match the sum with the answer.

1 + 1 = •	• 6
2 + 2 = •	• 8
3 + 3 = •	• 4
4 + 4 = •	• 16
5 + 5 = •	• 20
6 + 6 = •	• 2
7 + 7 = •	• 10
8 + 8 = •	• 14
9 + 9 = •	• 18
10 + 10 = •	• 12

2. Do these sums.

a 8 + 8 = ______ **b** 2 + 2 = ______

c 1 + 1 = ______ **d** 6 + 6 = ______

e 5 + 5 = ______ **f** 9 + 9 = ______

g 10 + 10 = ______ **h** 7 + 7 = ______

3. **a** What are 2 lots of 5? ______

b What are 2 lots of 7? ______

c What are 2 lots of 3? ______

4.

a How much are 2 pencils? ______

b How much are 2 rubbers? ______

c How much are 2 sharpeners? ______

d How much are 2 pads? ______

e How much are 2 pencils and 2 pads? ______

Subtraction 2

Remember ...

15 – 7 = 8

Here is a number strip to help you.

1	**2**	**3**	**4**	**5**	**6**	**7**	**8**	**9**	**10**	**11**	**12**	**13**	**14**	**15**	**16**	**17**	**18**	**19**	**20**

1. Try these sums.

a 20 – 6 = ______ **b** 9 – 6 = ______

c 17 – 7 = ______ **d** 18 – 9 = ______

e 12 – 8 = ______ **f** 16 – 7 = ______

g 15 – 10 = ______ **h** 14 – 6 = ______

2. Fill in the gaps. Couldnt do.

a 7 – ______ = 4 **b** 18 – ______ = 8

c 12 – 5 = ______ **d** 10 – ______ = 4

e ______ – 6 = 14 **f** ______ – 5 = 10

g 14 – 8 = ______ **h** 17 – ______ = 14

3. Do these sums. Remember you can use the number strip on page 28.

a 10 take away 6 = ______

b Take 14 from 20. ______

c 10 subtract 4 = ______

d Subtract 5 from 12. ______

e What number must I take from 20 to leave 10? ______

f What must I add to 12 to make 15? ______

g 13 add a number is 17. What is the number? ______

4. I had 20 sweets in a bag. I ate 7. How many sweets did I have left?

______

Then I ate 12 more! How many sweets do I have left now? ______

More than, less than

63	64	65	66	67	68	69	70	71	72	73	74	75	76	77	78	79	80	81	82	83	84	85	86	87	88

1. Use the number line.

a What is 1 more than 72? **73**

b What is 1 more than 79? ______

c What is 1 less than 67? ______

d What is 1 less than 83? ______

2. Answer these questions without using a number line.

a What is 1 more than 16? ______

b What is 1 less than 89? ______

c What is 1 more than 23? ______

d What is 1 less than 99? ______

3. Answer these questions. Use this number line.

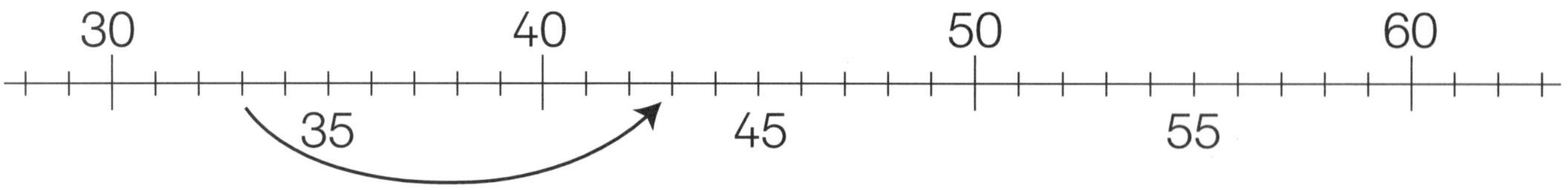

a What is 10 more than 33? **43**

b What is 10 more than 41? ______

c What is 10 less than 45? ______

4. Answer these questions.

a What is 10 less than 62? ______

b What is 10 more than 26? ______

c What is 10 less than 85? ______

5. Finish these number patterns.

a

3	**13**	**23**	**33**			**63**		

b

96	**86**	**76**			**46**			

6. Fill in the gaps.

a 32 $\xrightarrow{\text{10 more}}$ **42**

b ______ $\xrightarrow{\text{10 more}}$ 76

c 68 $\xrightarrow{\text{10 more}}$ ______

d ______ $\xrightarrow{\text{10 more}}$ 38

7. **a** I have saved 46p. Aziz has saved 10p more than me.
How much has Aziz saved? ______

b Pen has saved 78p. I have saved 10p less than her.
How much have I saved? ______

2 times table

5 lots of 2 is 10

oo + oo + oo + oo + oo = 10

2 2 2 2 2

5 × 2 = 10

× means 'lots of'

1. **a** 6 × 2 = oo + oo + oo + oo + oo + oo = ______

b 2 × 2 = oo + oo = ______

c 7 × 2 = oo + oo + oo + oo + oo + oo + oo = ______

d 1 × 2 = oo = ______

e 9 × 2 = oo + oo + oo + oo + oo + oo + oo + oo + oo = ______

f 3 × 2 = oo + oo + oo = ______

g 5 × 2 = oo + oo + oo + oo + oo = ______

h 4 × 2 = oo + oo + oo + oo = ______

2. $1 \times 2 =$ ______

$2 \times 2 =$ ______

$3 \times 2 =$ ______

$4 \times 2 =$ ______

$5 \times 2 =$ ______

$6 \times 2 =$ ______

$7 \times 2 =$ ______

$8 \times 2 =$ ______

$9 \times 2 =$ ______

$10 \times 2 =$ ______

3. Fill in the gaps.

a $4 \times 2 =$ ______

b $3 \times 2 =$ ______

c ______ $\times 2 = 2$

d ______ $\times 2 = 12$

e $8 \times$ ______ $= 16$

f $5 \times$ ______ $= 10$

g ______ $\times 2 = 20$

h $3 \times$ ______ $= 6$

i $7 \times 2 =$ ______

j ______ $\times 2 = 18$

k ______ $\times 2 = 8$

l $1 \times$ ______ $= 2$

4. Finish the 2 times table lists.

a

2	**4**		**8**	**10**		**14**	**16**	

b

	4		**8**		**12**		**16**	

Division 1

Divide 6 sweets between Emma and Rob.

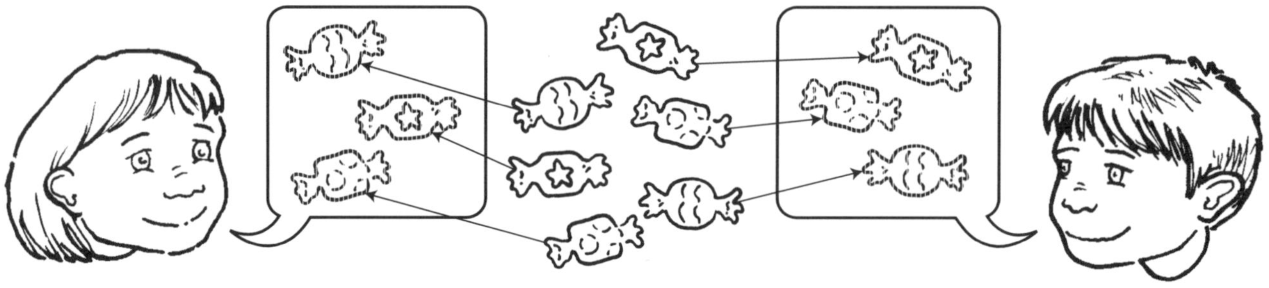

6 sweets **shared by** 2 = 3 each.

1. **a** Share 8 sweets between 2 children.

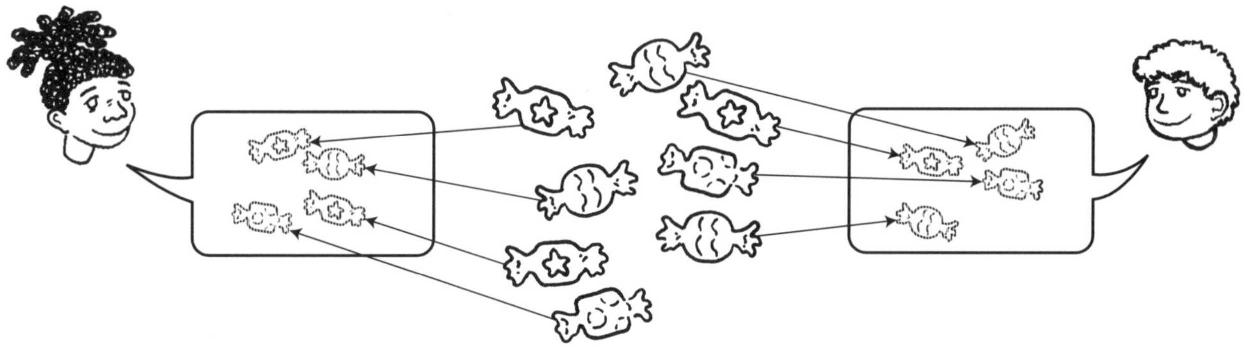

How many do they have each? ______ each.

b Share 12 sweets between 3 children.

How many do they have each?

______ each.

If we divide 6 sweets between 2 children they get 3 sweets each.
We write the sum like this ... **6 ÷ 2 = 3**

÷ means divide or share

2. Answer these sums. Share the numbers into the boxes if you like.

a 4 ÷ 2 = **2**

○ ○ ○ ○
☐ ☐

b 9 ÷ 3 = ______

○ ○ ○ ○ ○ ○ ○ ○ ○
☐ ☐ ☐

c 10 ÷ 5 = ______

○ ○ ○ ○ ○ ○ ○ ○ ○ ○
☐ ☐ ☐ ☐ ☐

d 8 ÷ 2 = ______

○ ○ ○ ○ ○ ○ ○ ○
☐ ☐

3. Brian had nine sweets. He shared them with two of his friends, John and Sean. How many did they have each?

______ Brian

______ John

______ Sean

Measuring in cms and ms

You will need a ruler.

Sometimes we measure **length** using **metres** (m) and sometimes we use **centimetres** (cm).

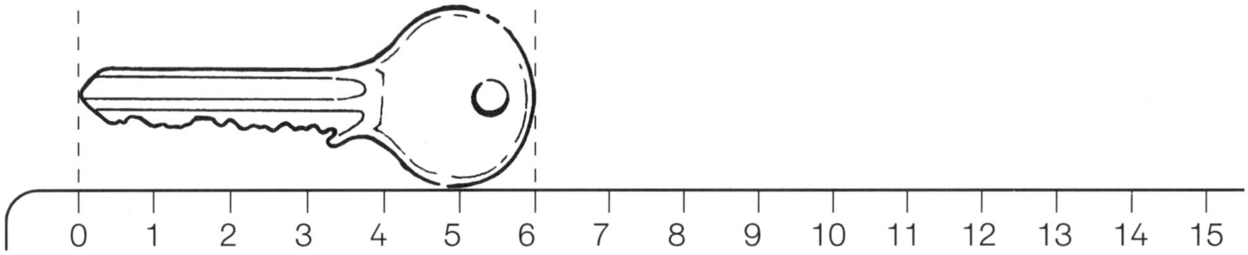

This key is 6 centimetres long.

We can write centimetres as **cm**.

1. Measure these pencils using a ruler. Look carefully at the first one.

a
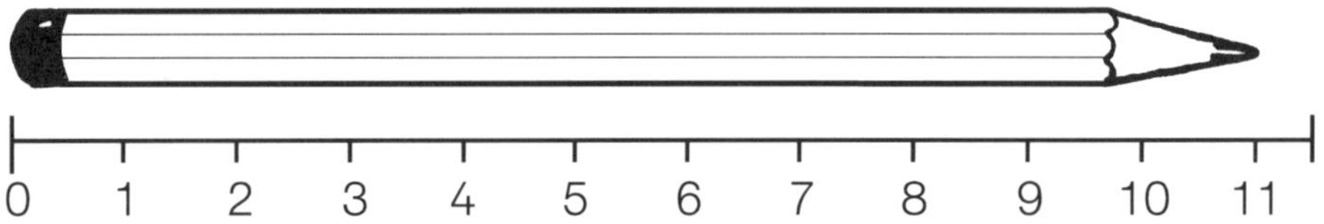

= **11** cm

b
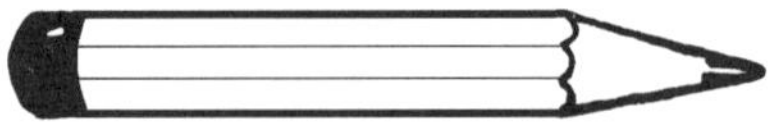
_____ cm

c
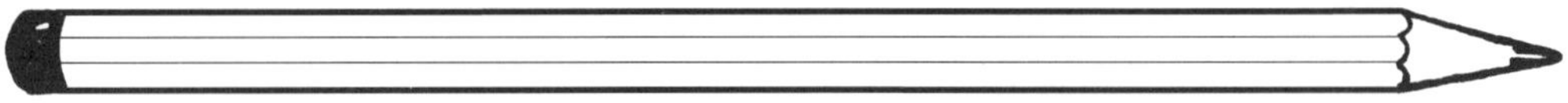
_____ cm

d
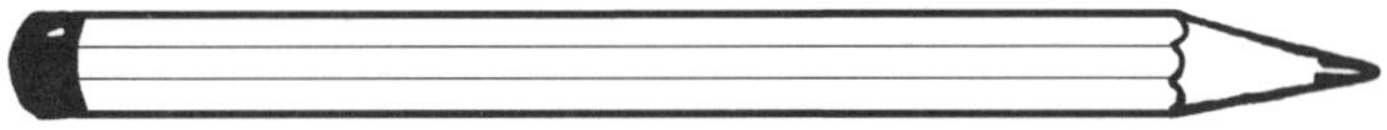
_____ cm

e
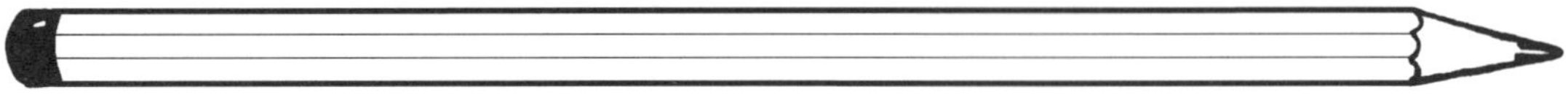
_____ cm

f
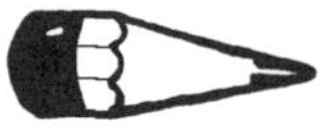
_____ cm

100 centimetres (cm) = 1 metre (m)

0 10 20 30 40 50 60 70 80 90 100 **cm**

m

To measure big objects like a door or a car we use **metres (m)**.

3 m

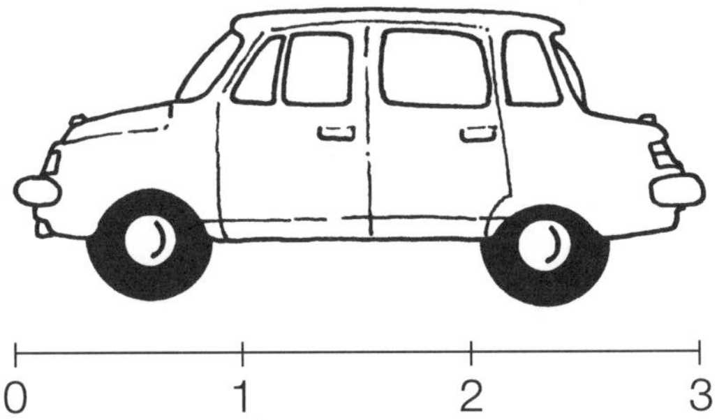

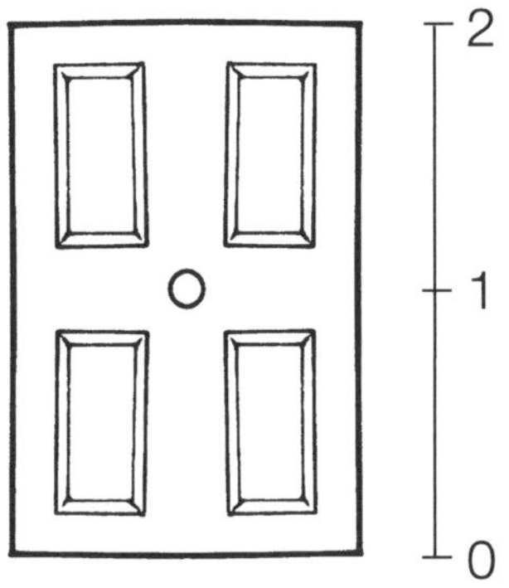

2 m

2. Answer these questions.

a How many cm are in one m? ______ cm

b Would we use m or cm to measure a garden? ______

c Would we use m or cm to measure a playground? ______

3. Would we use cm or m to measure ...

a a rubber? ______

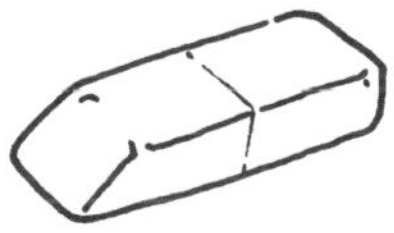

b a book? ______

c a tree? ______

d a foot? ______

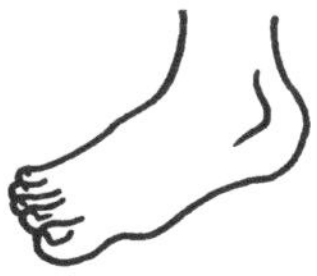

e a lorry? ______

f a pencil? ______

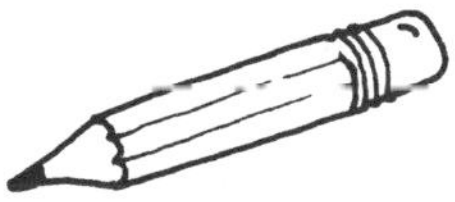

g a train? ______

h a road? ______

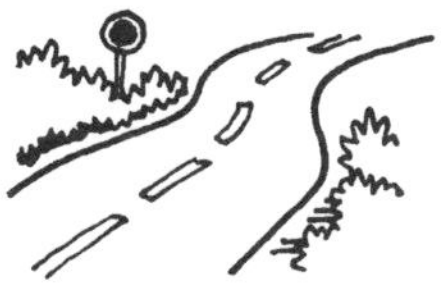

Drawing straight lines

1. Can you draw a straight line between these dots?

a

b

c

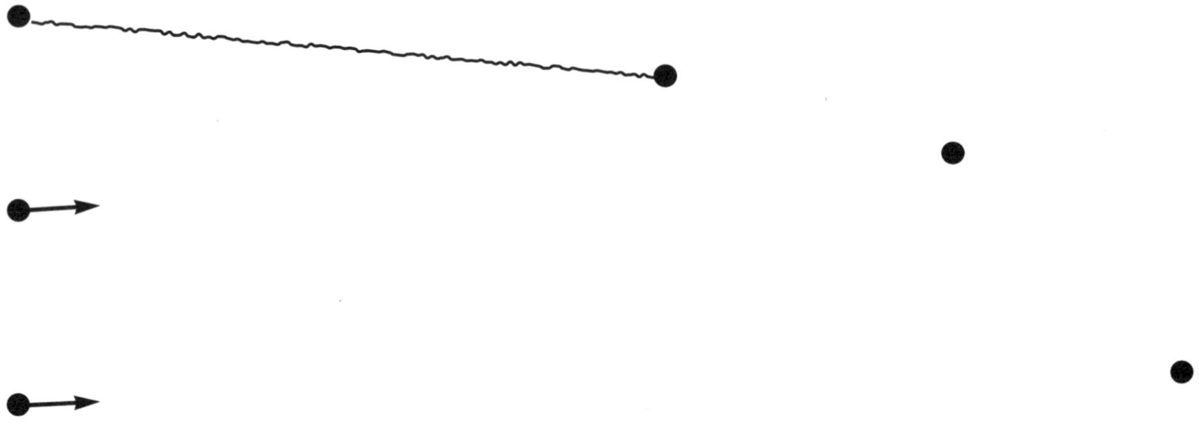

We can make our lines straight using a **ruler**.

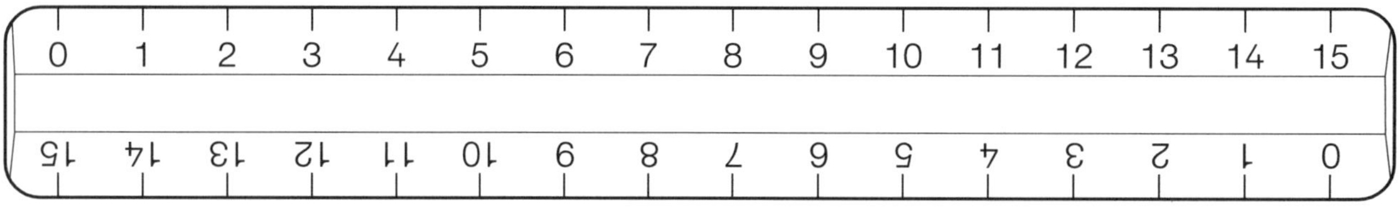

2. Draw a line between these dots using a ruler.

a

b

c

d

Remember ...
we measure cms with a ruler.

3. Draw a straight line between the dots and measure it.

a 

_______ cm

b • • _______ cm

c • • _______ cm

d • • _______ cm

e • • _______ cm

f • • _______ cm

4. Measure these lines.

a 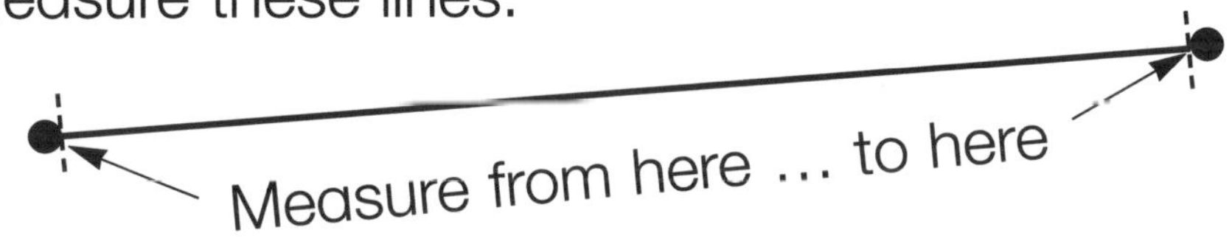

_______ cm

b 
_______ cm

c 
_______ cm

d 
_______ cm

Fractions – thirds

Look at this cake.

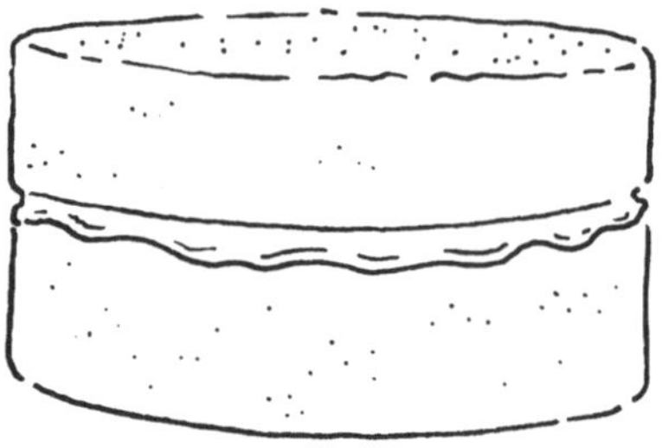

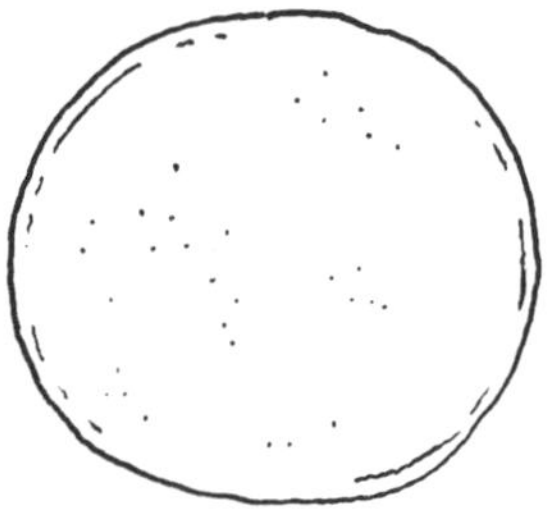

If we cut it into 3 **equal** bits it looks like this.

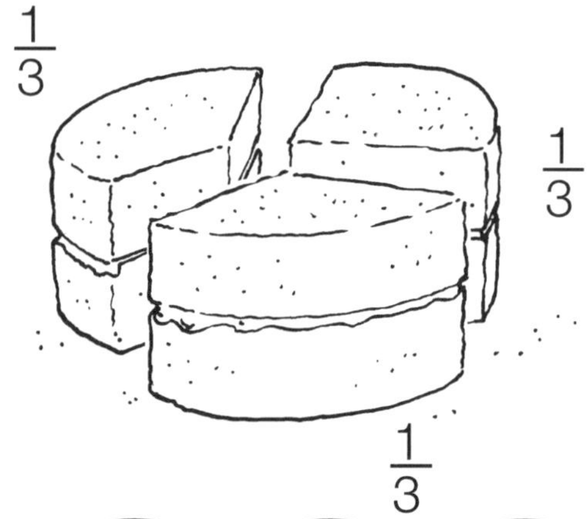

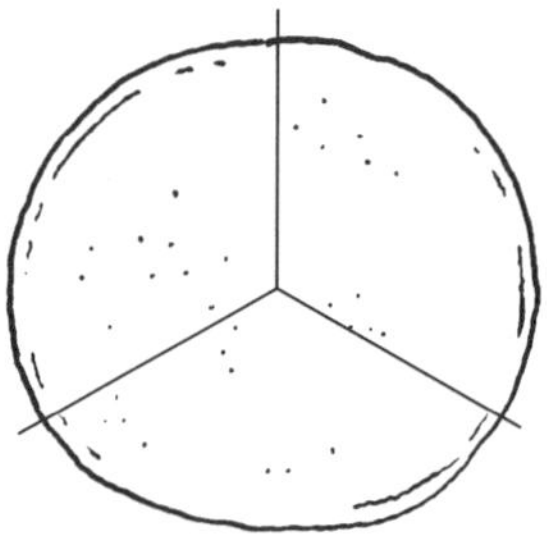

1. Cut these things into thirds.

a

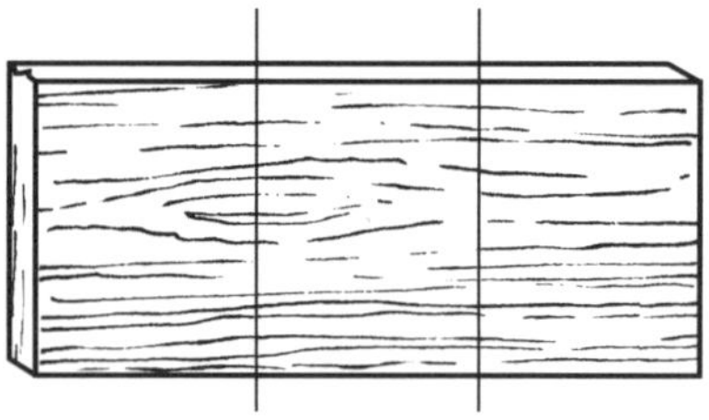

b

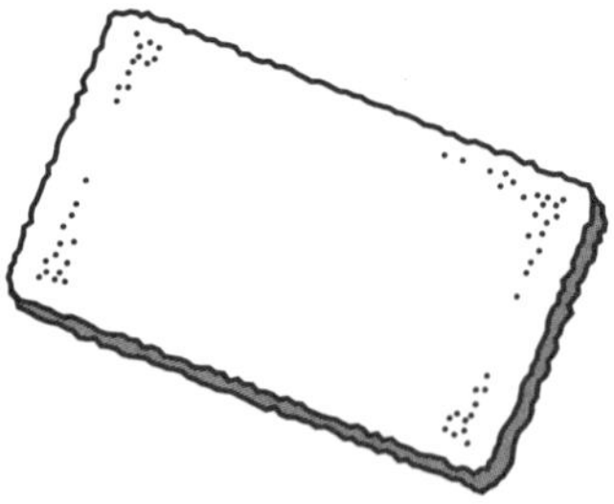

c

We write a third like this ... $\mathbf{\frac{1}{3}}$.

Shapes can be cut into $\frac{1}{3}$ s using two lines like this ...

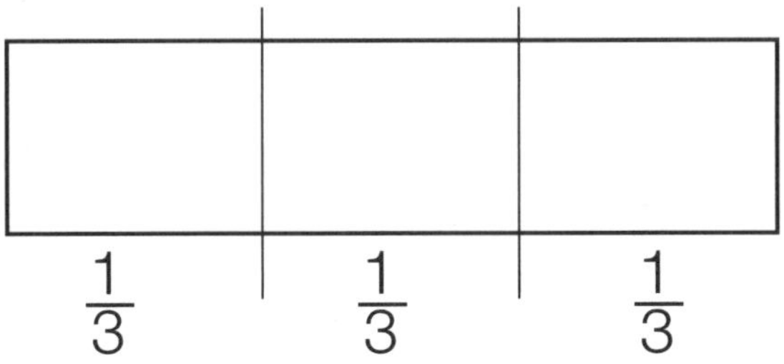

Remember ...
it is cut into **equal** bits.

2. Cut these shapes into $\frac{1}{3}$s.

a **b** **c**

3. Tick and colour the shapes that have been cut in $\frac{1}{3}$s.

a **b** **c** **d**

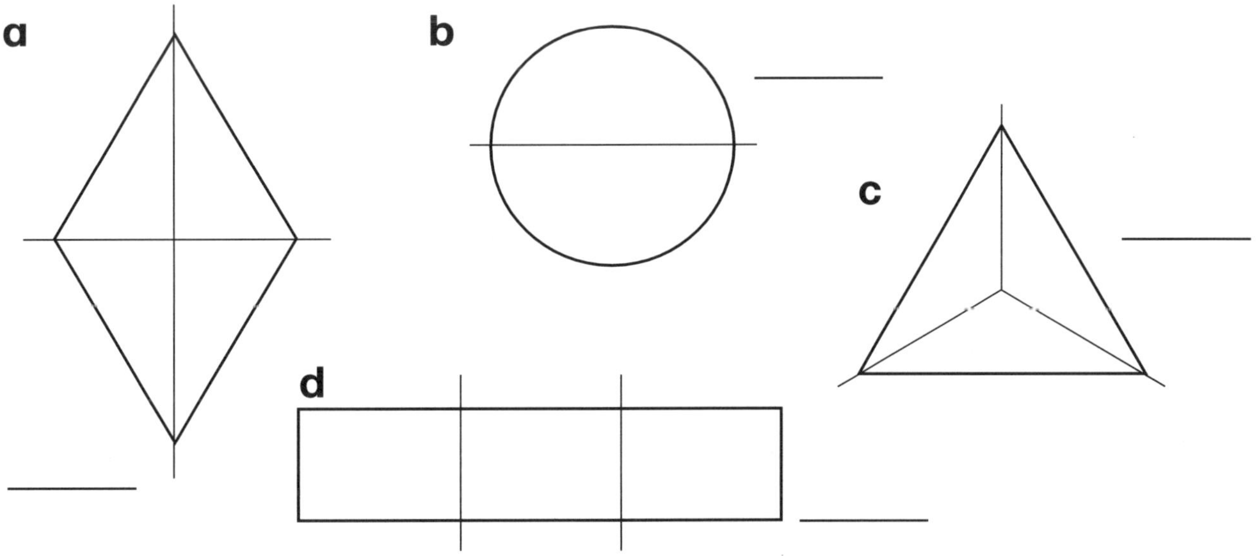

Check-up 2

1. What is the time?

a

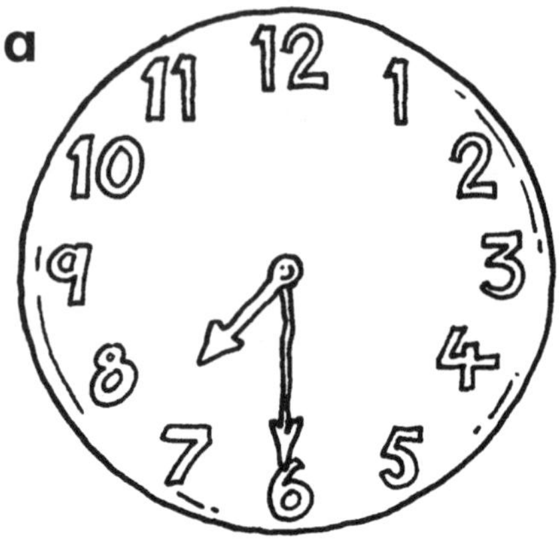

$\frac{1}{2}$ past ______

b

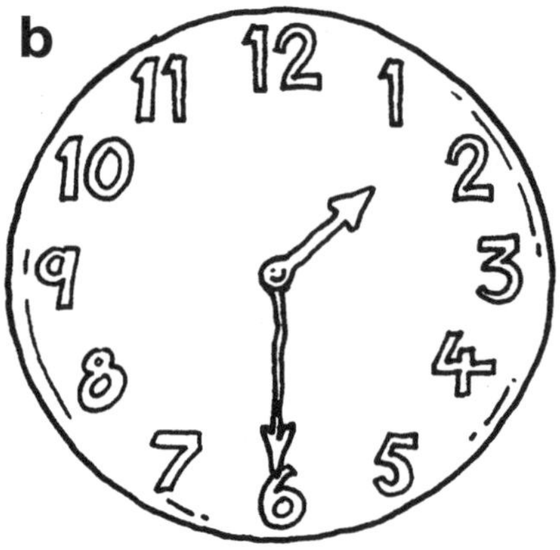

$\frac{1}{2}$ past ______

c

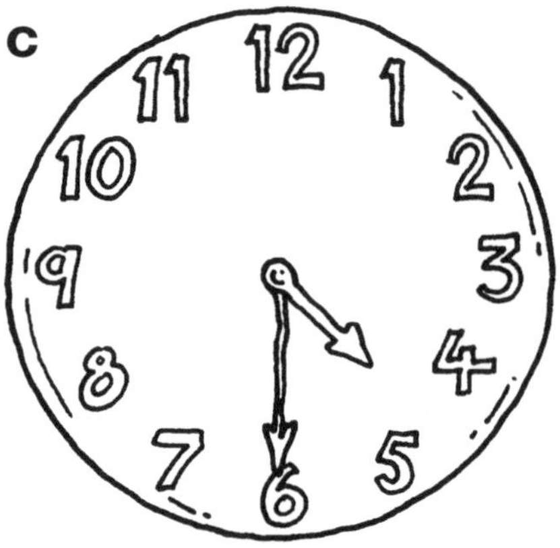

$\frac{1}{2}$ past ______

2. **a** 5 + 5 = ______

b 2 + 2 = ______

c 8 + 8 = ______

d 10 + 10 = ______

3. **a** Take 15 from 20. ______

b Subtract 14 from 19. ______

c 12 add a number is 14. What is the number? ______

d Subtract 12 from 16. ______

4. **a** What is 10 more than 57? ______

b What is 10 less than 23? ______

c What is 10 less than 86? ______

d What is 10 more than 1? ______

5. **a** 3 × 2 = ______ **b** 8 × 2 = ______

c 6 × 2 = ______ **d** 9 × 2 = ______

6.

a 10 ÷ 5 = ______

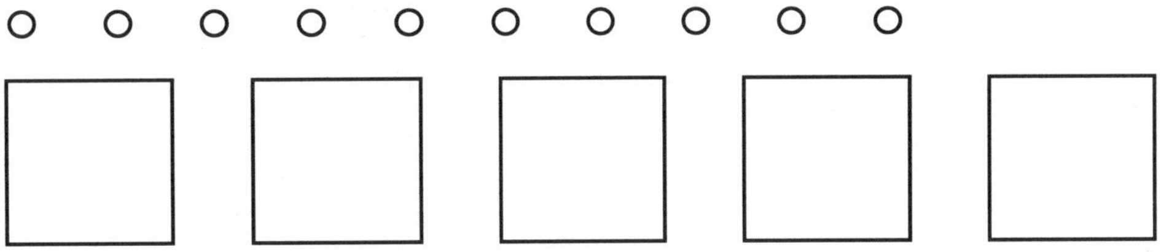

b 6 ÷ 3 = ______

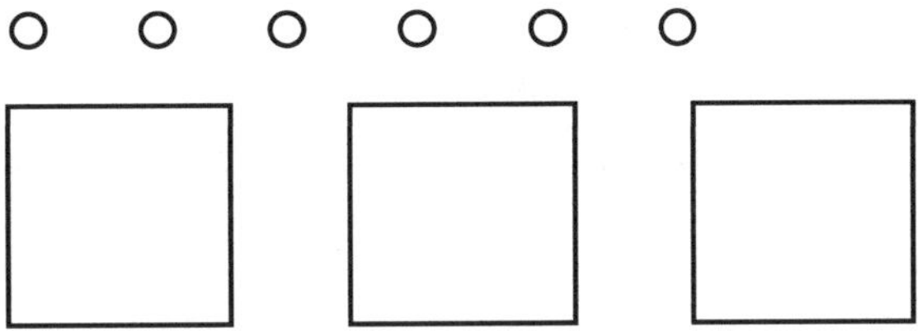

7. What would we use to measure? cm or m?

a a flower ______ **b** a lorry ______

8. Draw a straight red line between the dots and measure it with a ruler.

a

______ cm

b ● ● ______ cm

c ● ● ______ cm

9. Tick and colour the shapes that have been cut in $\frac{1}{3}$s.

a

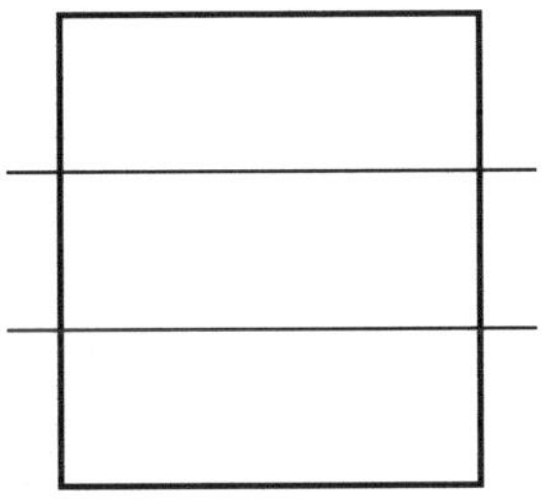

______

b

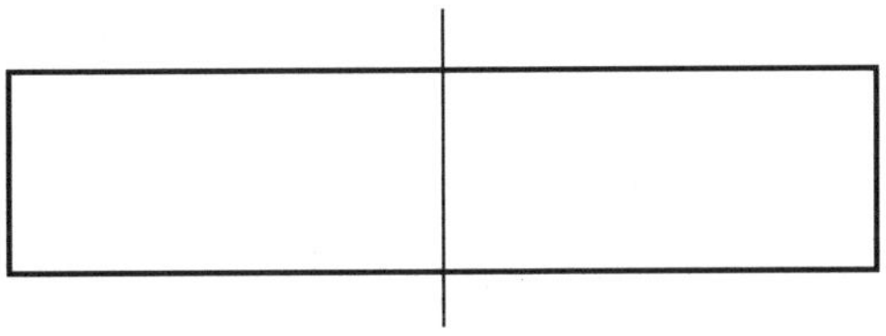

______

c

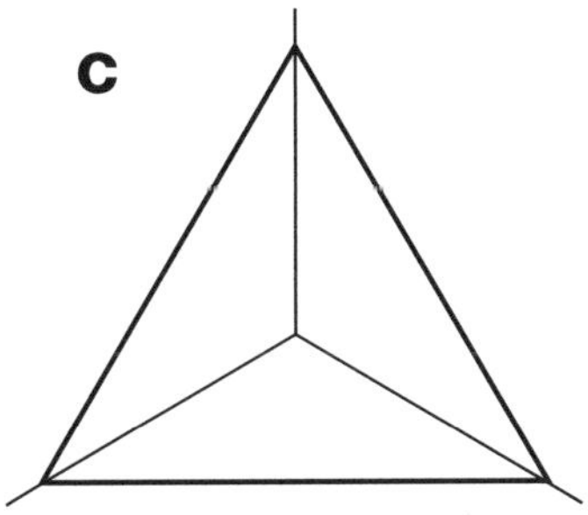

______

More than, less than, in between

1. Do you remember ...

a What is 1 more than 31? ______

b What is 10 less than 40? ______

c What is 10 more than 63? ______

25	26	27	28	29	30	31	32	33	34	35	36	37	38	39	40	41	42	43	44

2. Which is less?

a 28 or 25? **25**

b 25 or 35? ______

c 44 or 37? ______

d 37 or 38? ______

3. Which is more?

a 30 or 39? ______

b 39 or 29? ______

c 37 or 38? ______

d 40 or 39? ______

4. Now try these without using a number line.

Which is less?

a 36 or 63? ______

b 68 or 86? ______

c 24 or 42? ______

d 11 or 19? ______

Which is more?

e 38 or 72? ______

f 28 or 18? ______

g 44 or 55? ______

h 87 or 78? ______

56	**57**	**58**	**59**	**60**	**61**	**62**	**63**	**64**	**65**	**66**	**67**	**68**	**69**	**70**	**71**	**72**	**73**	**74**	**75**

Look at the numbers 64 and 69. Four numbers lie **between** them. These are 65, 66, 67, 68.

5. Write the two numbers that lie between ...

a 57 ______ ______ 60

b 78 ______ ______ 81

c 28 ______ ______ 31

d 16 ______ ______ 19

e 50 ______ ______ 53

f 91 ______ ______ 94

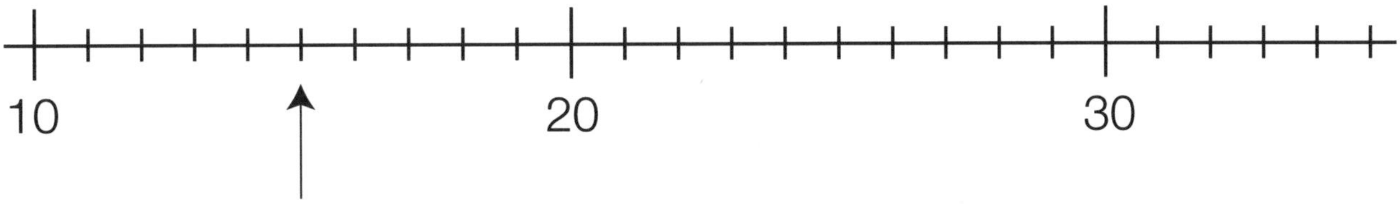

6. a Which number is halfway between 10 and 20? ______

b Which number is halfway between 20 and 30? ______

7. Answer these questions.

a The bun cost 1p more than 19p and 1p less than 21p.

How much did it cost? ______

b The string is 2 cm longer than 27 cm and 2 cm shorter than 31 cm.

How long is it? ______

c The sweets cost halfway between 10p and 14p.

What did they cost? ______

Pairs of numbers to 20

Here are three ways we can make 20 ...

13 + 7 = 20 **6 + 14 = 20** **11 + 9 = 20**

1. Finish these sums.

a 1 + **19** = 20 **b** ______ + 6 = 20

c ______ + 11 = 20 **d** 3 + ______ = 20

e 5 + ______ = 20 **f** 8 + = ______ 20

g 13 + ______ = 20 **h** ______ + 9 = 20

i ______ + 2 = 20 **j** 10 + ______ = 20

k 7 + ______ = 20 **l** ______ + 4 = 20

2. Check these sums. ✔ = right ✘ = wrong

a 15 + 14 = 20	✘	**b** 12 + 7 = 20	
c 9 + 11 = 20		**d** 18 + 3 = 20	
e 6 + 14 = 20		**f** 11 + 8 = 20	
g 8 + 12 = 20		**h** 10 + 9 = 20	
i 19 + 0 = 20		**j** 5 + 15 = 20	

3. Finish these sums.

a 20 − 7 = ______

b 20 − 9 = ______

c 20 − 3 = ______

d 20 − 16 = ______

e 20 − 20 = ______

f 20 − 6 = ______

g 20 − 5 = ______

h 20 − 17 = ______

i 20 − 19 = ______

j 20 − 8 = ______

4. Check these sums. ✔ = right ✘ = wrong

a 20 − 17 = 4 ☐

b 20 − 5 = 15 ☐

c 20 − 8 = 13 ☐

d 20 − 6 = 14 ☐

5. Match the cards so they total 20.

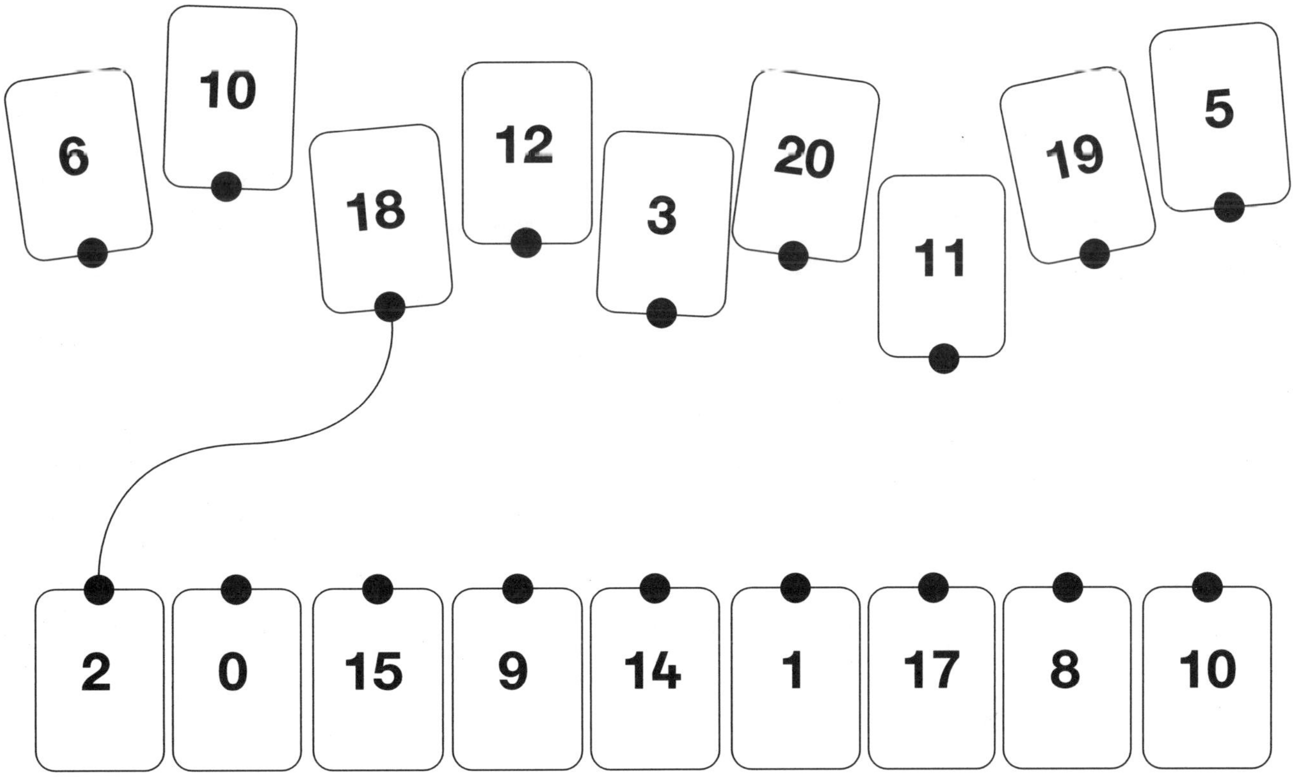

Money

Look at these coins ...

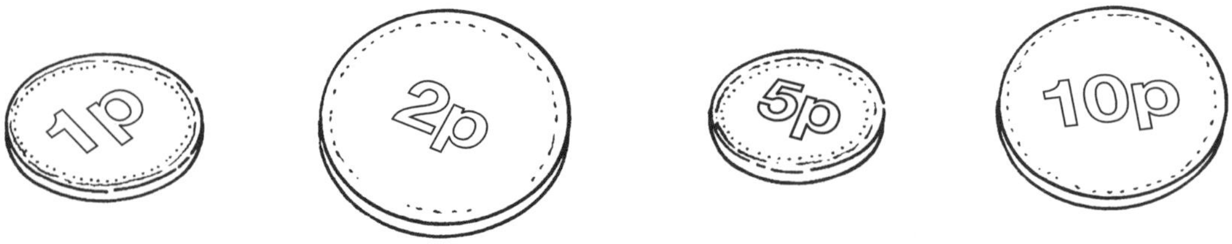

1. Draw in the money bags the coins that need to be added together to make ...

a 6p

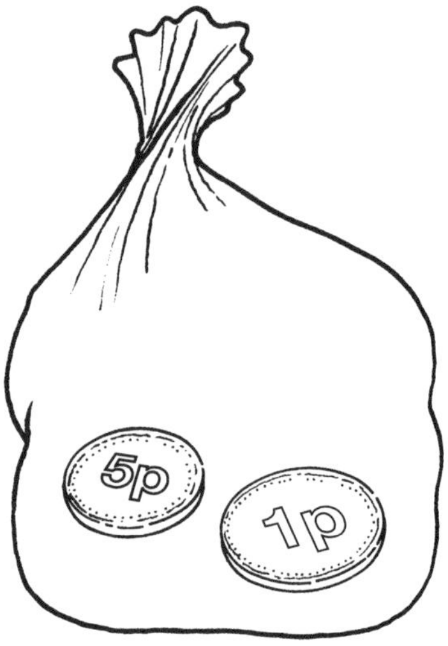

b 7p

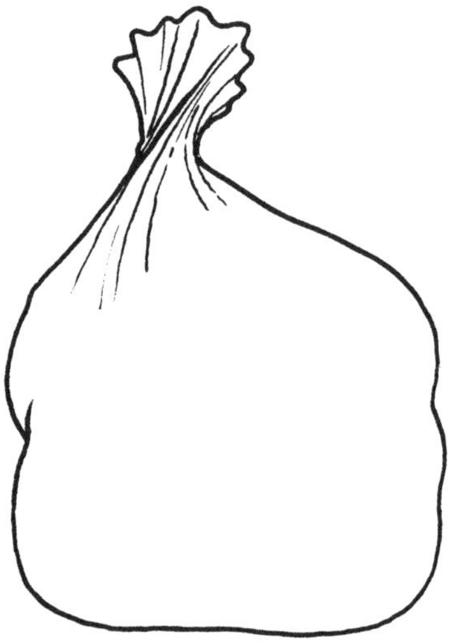

c 15p

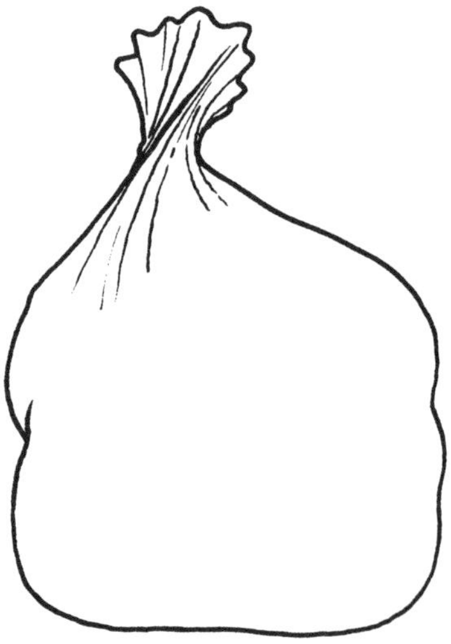

d 11p

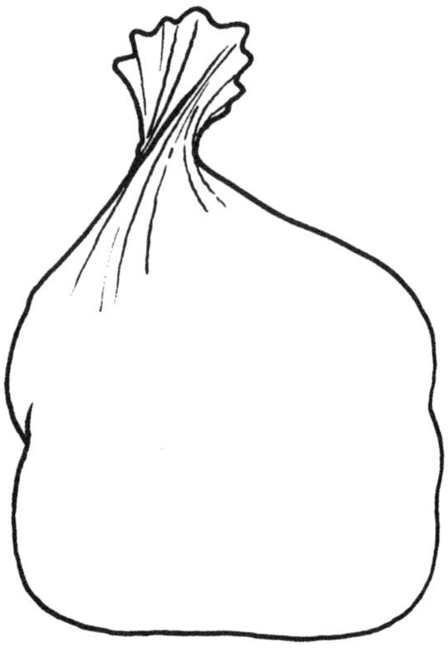

e 8p

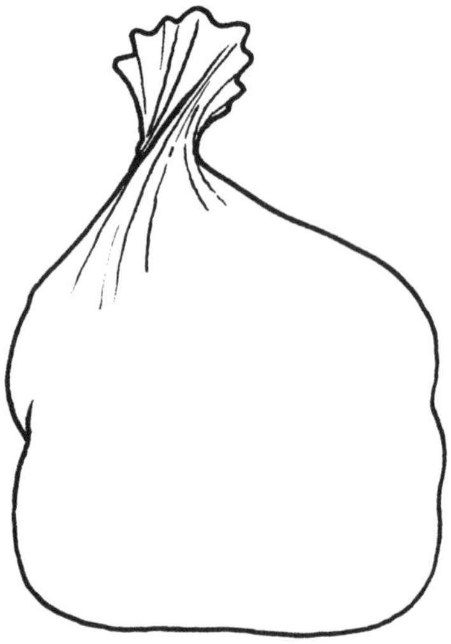

f 13p

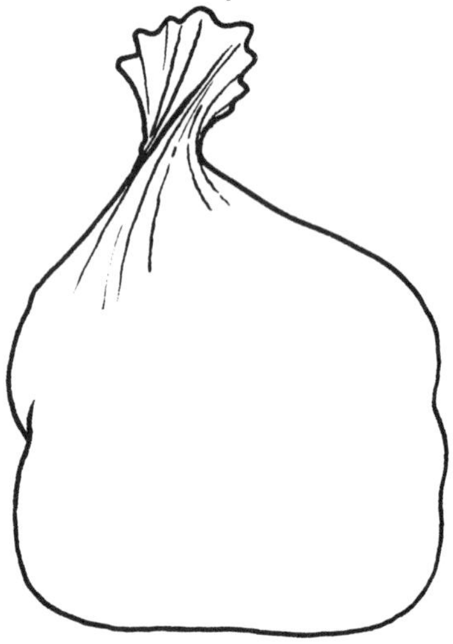

Here are two more coins we use.

2. Now write a sum showing which coins you would use.

a 72p = **50** p + **20** p + **2** p

b 60p = ______ p + ______ p

c 25p = ______ p + ______ p

d 55p = ______ p + ______ p

e 21p = ______ p + ______ p

f 32p = ______ p + ______ p + ______ p

3. **a** Anil spent 5p on sweets. What was his change from 10p?

______ p

b Rosie had 15p. She spent 5p. How much did she have left?

______ p

c Tim spent 5p and 2p on stickers. What was his change from 10p?

______ p

5 times table

3 lots of 5 is 15

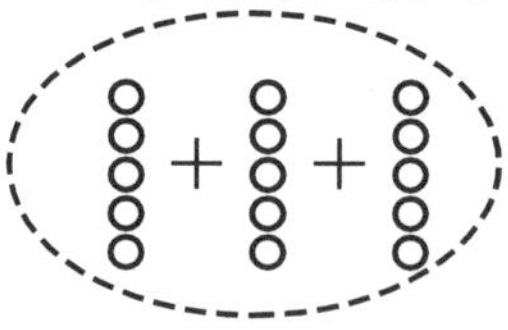 = 15

5 5 5

3 × 5 = **15**

× means 'lots of'

1. a 6 × 5 = 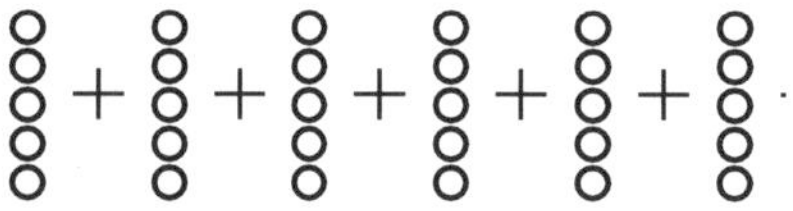 = ______

b 9 × 5 = 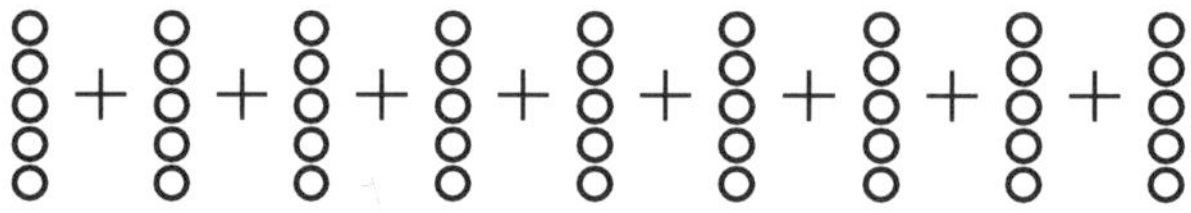 = ______

c 2 × 5 = 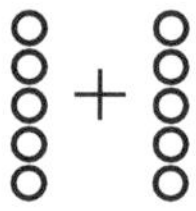 = ______

d 5 × 5 = 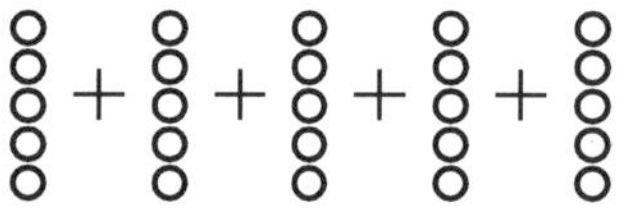 = ______

e 10 × 5 = 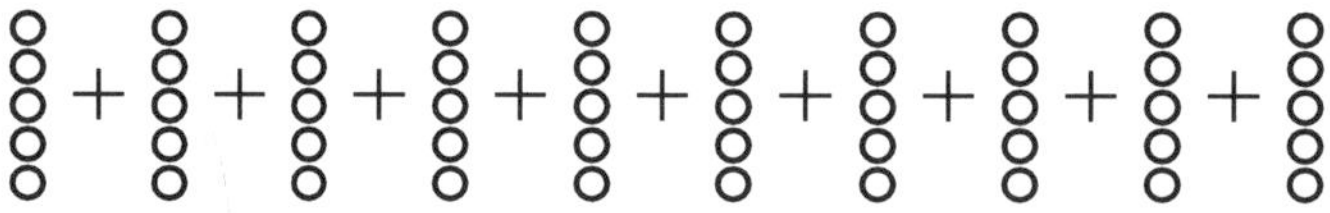 = ______

f 1 × 5 =  = ______

g 7 × 5 = 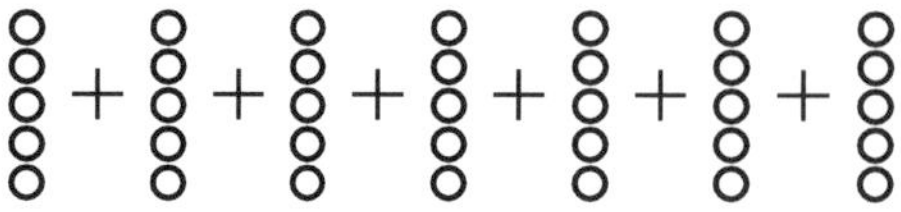 = ______

h 4 × 5 = 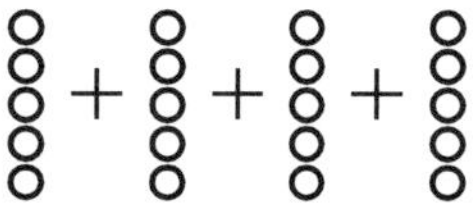 = ______

2. 1 × 5 = ______

2 × 5 = ______

3 × 5 = ______

4 × 5 = ______

5 × 5 = ______

6 × 5 = ______

7 × 5 = ______

8 × 5 = ______

9 × 5 = ______

10 × 5 = ______

3. Fill in the gaps.

a 6 × 5 = ______

b ______ × 5 = 30

c 2 × 5 = ______

d 10 × ______ = 50

e ______ × 5 = 40

f ______ × 5 = 15

g ______ × 5 = 20

h 7 × 5 = ______

i 9 × ______ = 45

j 5 × ______ = 25

k ______ × 5 = 10

l 1 × 5 = ______

4. Finish the 5 times table lists.

a

5	**10**			**25**		**35**			**50**

b

	10		**20**			**35**		**45**	

Division 2 – with remainders

Divide 7 sweets between Emma and Rob.

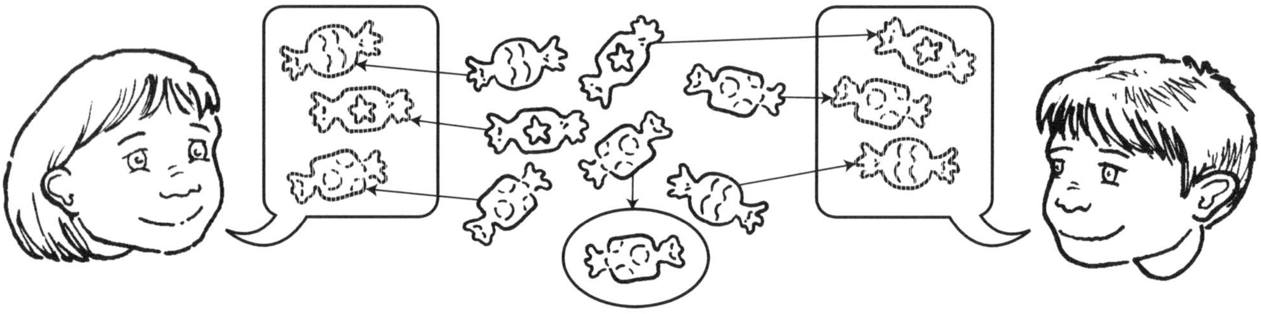

7 sweets shared by 2 = 3 each with 1 left over.

We say there is a **remainder** of 1.

1. Share 5 sweets between 2 children. What is left over?

a

How many do they have each? ______ each

______ remainder

b Share 17 sweets between 3 children.

How many do they have each?

______ each

______ remainder

We write division (sharing) sums like this ...

7 ÷ 2 = 3 r 1.

r = remainder

2. Do these sums.

a 7 ÷ 3 = = ___ r ___

b 9 ÷ 4 = = ___ r ___

c 13 ÷ 3 = = ___ r ___

d 14 ÷ 2 = = ___ r ___

e 11 ÷ 2 = = ___ r ___

3. Richard had a bag of sixteen sweets. He shared them with his brothers, James and Matthew.

How many will they have each? ______

What is the remainder? ______

Rounding to the nearest 10

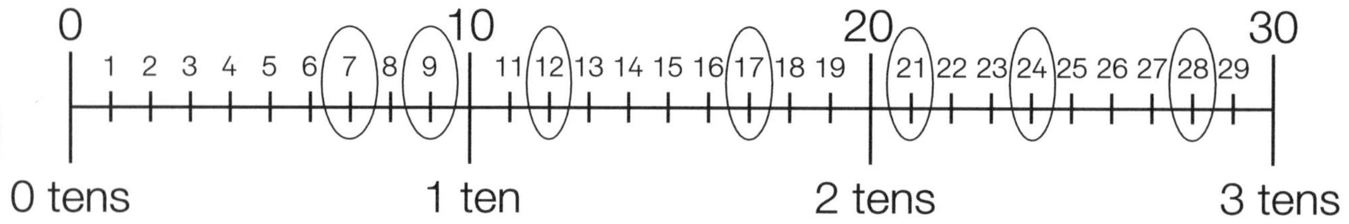

1. Look at the number line.

- **a** Is 9 closer to the number 0 or 10? **10**
- **b** Is 17 closer to the number 10 or 20? ______
- **c** Is 12 closer to the number 10 or 20? ______
- **d** Is 24 closer to the number 20 or 30? ______
- **e** Is 28 closer to the number 20 or 30? ______
- **f** Is 21 closer to the number 20 or 30? ______
- **g** Is 7 closer to the number 10 or 20? ______

Look at the number line again. Find the number 19.
It is closer to the number 20 than the number 10.
We say 19 is closer to 20 *or* **the nearest ten to 19 is 20.**

2. Look at the number line and fill in the gaps.

a The nearest ten to 13 is ______ .

b The nearest ten to 21 is ______ .

c The nearest ten to 7 is ______ .

d The nearest ten to 18 is ______ .

e The nearest ten to 28 is ______ .

f The nearest ten to 16 is ______ .

g The nearest ten to 24 is ______ .

3. Deano ran in a race. He took 9 seconds.
Tim took 17 seconds.
Pen took 12 seconds.

a Deano and Pen each took about ______ seconds, rounded to the nearest ten.

b Tim took about ______ seconds rounded to the nearest ten.

Counting in steps

Look at the frog. It is jumping along a number line.

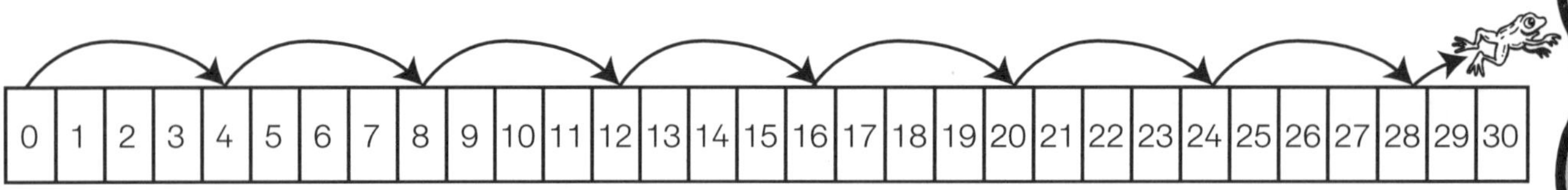

The frog jumps up 4 numbers each time.

1. How many numbers does the frog jump up each time?

a

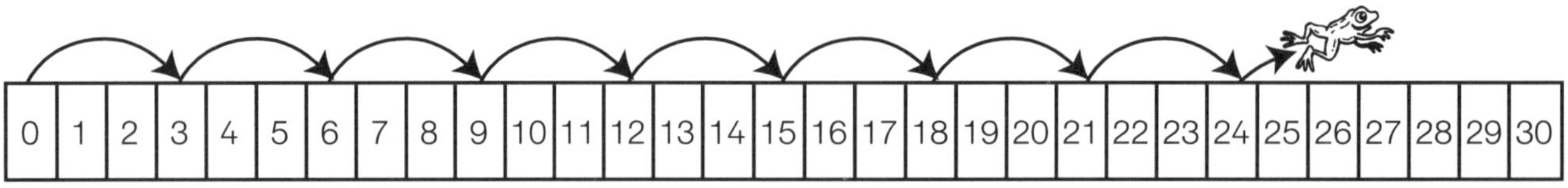

______ numbers each time

b

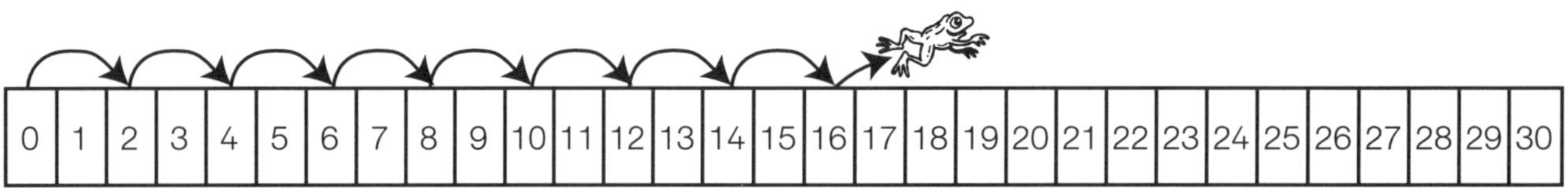

______ numbers each time

c

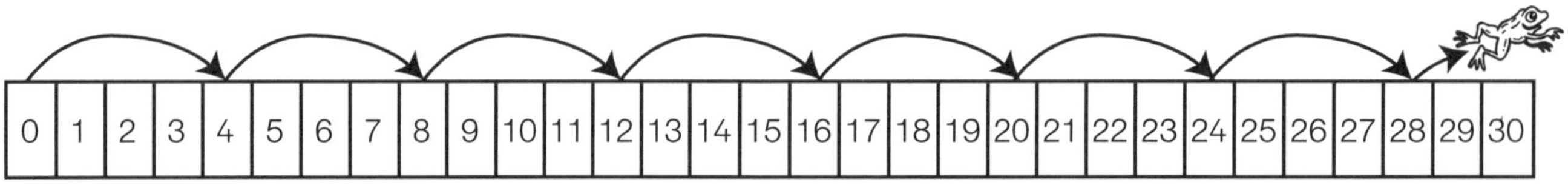

______ numbers each time

2. Finish the jumps keeping them the same.

a

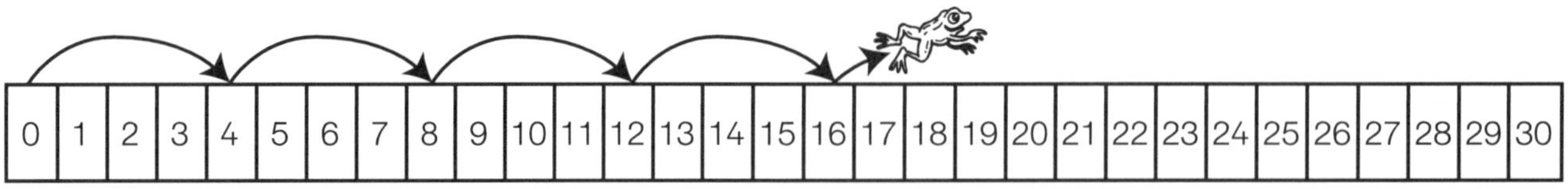

b

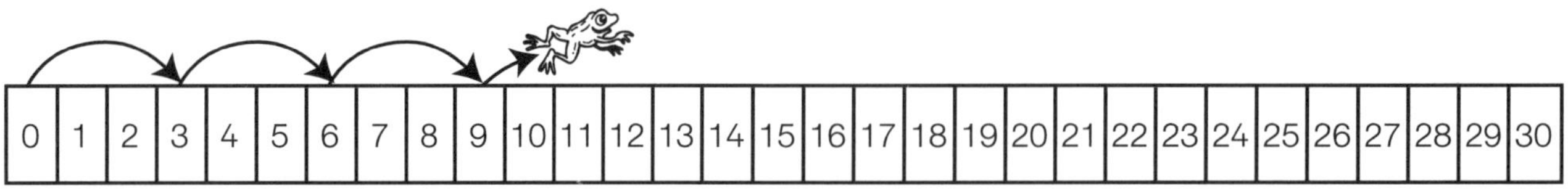

3. Which numbers come next?

a 4   8   12   16 ______ ______ ______

b 5   10   15 ______ ______ ______ ______

c 2   4   6 ______ ______ ______ ______

d 3   6   9 ______ ______ ______ ______

4. Fill in the missing numbers.

a 4 ______ ______ 16 ______ 24

b ______ 6 ______ 12 ______ 18

c 2 ______ ______ 8 ______ ______

5. Colour blue the numbers that go up by 3 each time.

1	2	3	4	5	6
7	8	9	10	11	12
13	14	15	16	17	18
19	20	21	22	23	24

What do you notice?

____

____

Fractions – $\frac{1}{2}$ $\frac{1}{4}$ $\frac{1}{3}$

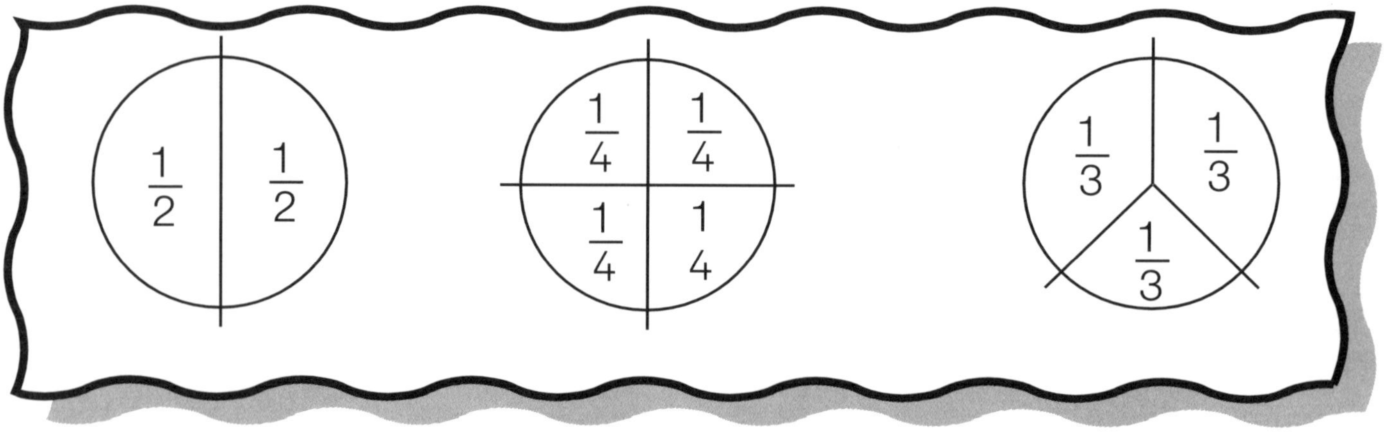

1. Which is bigger?

a $\frac{1}{2}$ or $\frac{1}{4}$? **$\frac{1}{2}$**  or 

b $\frac{1}{4}$ or $\frac{1}{3}$? ______  or 

c $\frac{1}{2}$ or $\frac{1}{3}$? ______  or 

2. Look at the circles at the top of the page.

a How many $\frac{1}{2}$ s in 1 whole circle? **2** $\frac{1}{2}$ s

b How many $\frac{1}{4}$ s in 1 whole circle? ______ $\frac{1}{4}$ s

c How many $\frac{1}{3}$ s in 1 whole circle? ______ $\frac{1}{3}$ s

3. a $\frac{1}{4}$ and $\frac{1}{4}$ = **$\frac{2}{4}$**

b $\frac{1}{3}$ and $\frac{1}{3}$ = $\frac{\quad}{3}$

c $\frac{1}{4}$ and $\frac{1}{4}$ and $\frac{1}{4}$ = $\frac{\quad}{4}$

4. Colour the fraction red.

a

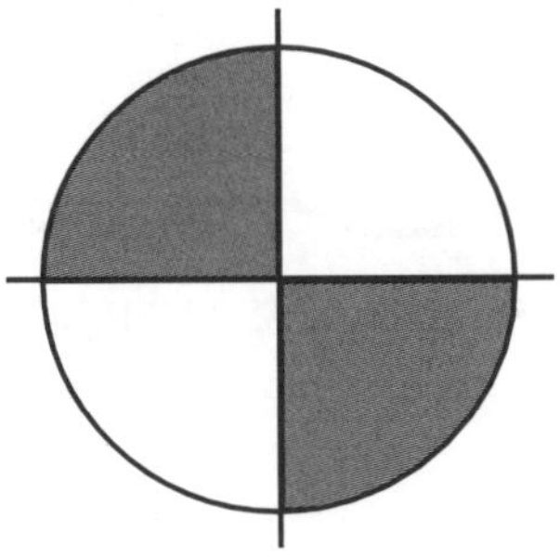

$\frac{1}{4} + \frac{1}{4} = \frac{2}{4}$

b

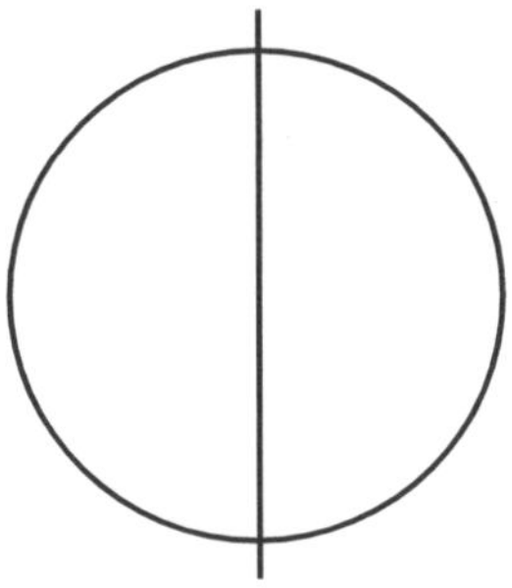

$\frac{1}{2}$

c

$\frac{1}{3} + \frac{1}{3} = \frac{2}{3}$

d

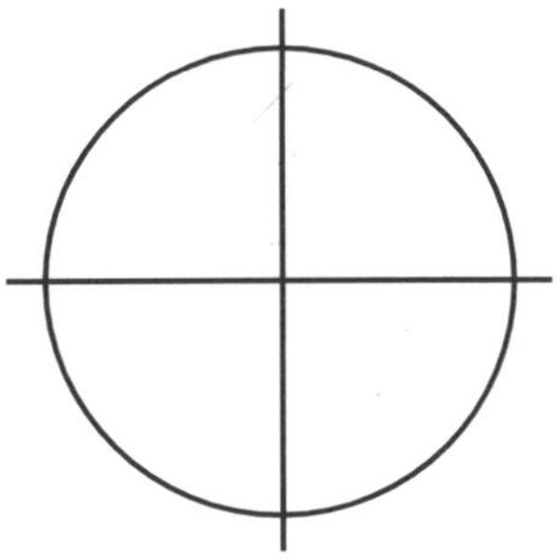

$\frac{1}{4} + \frac{1}{4} + \frac{1}{4} = \frac{3}{4}$

5. Which is smaller? Think carefully.

a $\frac{1}{2}$ or $\frac{1}{4}$ ______

b $\frac{3}{4}$ or $\frac{1}{2}$ ______

c $\frac{2}{4}$ or $\frac{1}{3}$ ______

d $\frac{1}{2}$ or $\frac{2}{3}$ ______

6. Put these numbers in order, starting with the biggest.

a $\frac{1}{4}$ $\frac{1}{3}$ $\frac{1}{2}$ $\frac{1}{2}$ ______ ______

b $\frac{1}{2}$ $\frac{2}{3}$ $\frac{1}{4}$ ______ ______ ______

Estimate to 100

Another way of saying 'guess which number' is '**estimate** which number'.

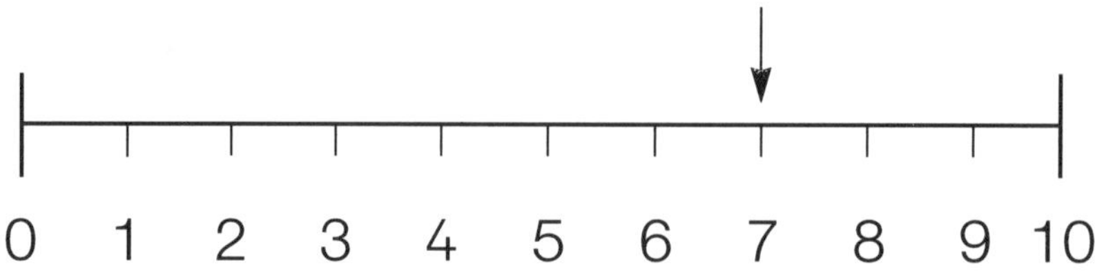

I estimate the arrow is pointing at the number 7.

1. Estimate which number the arrow is pointing at.

a
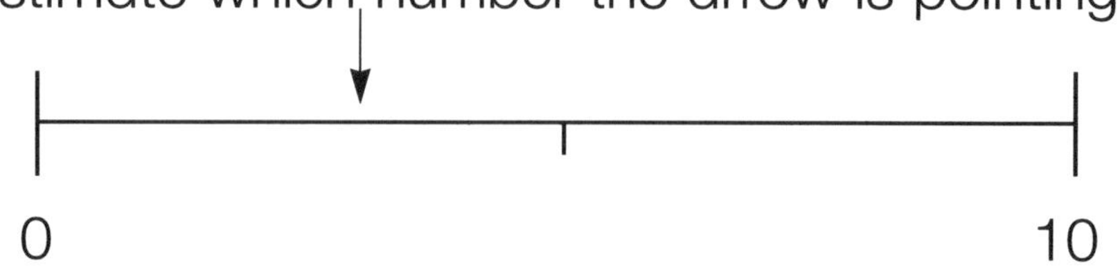

3

b
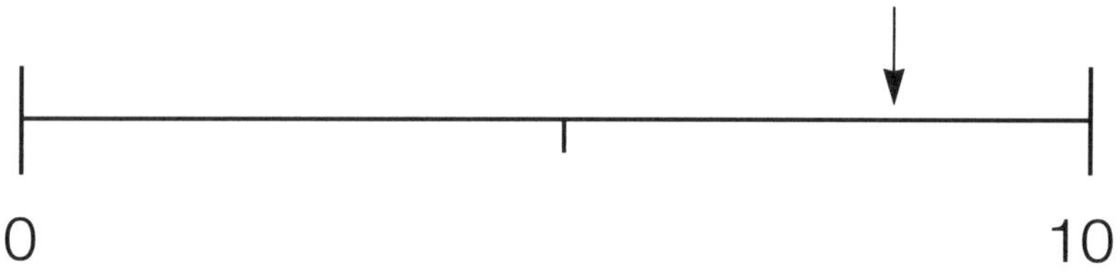

______

c
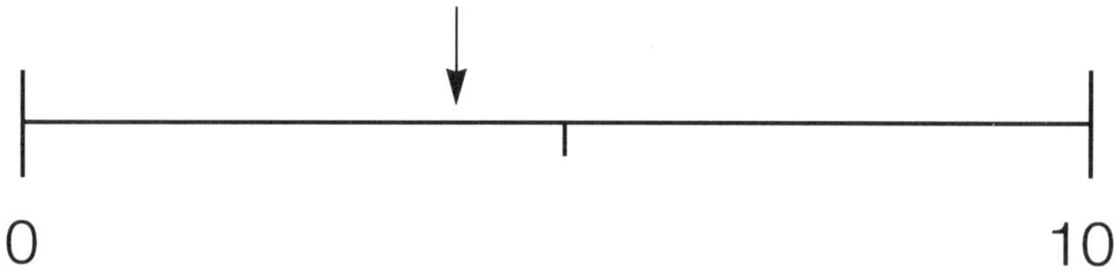

______

d
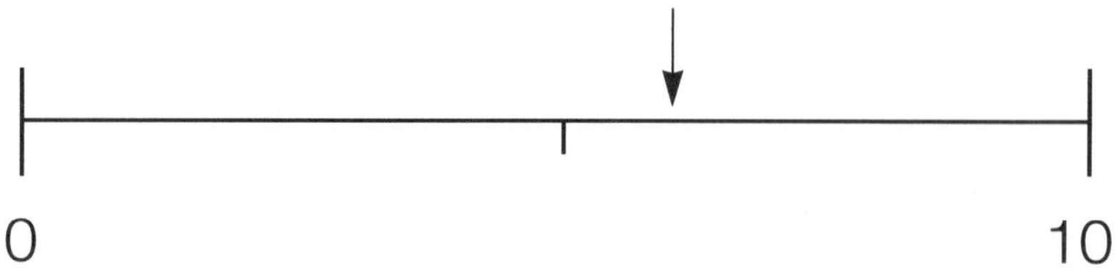

______

e
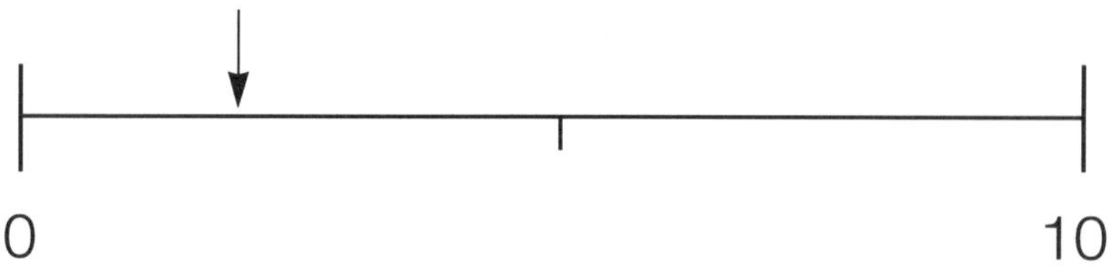

______

2. Estimate which number the arrow is pointing at.

a 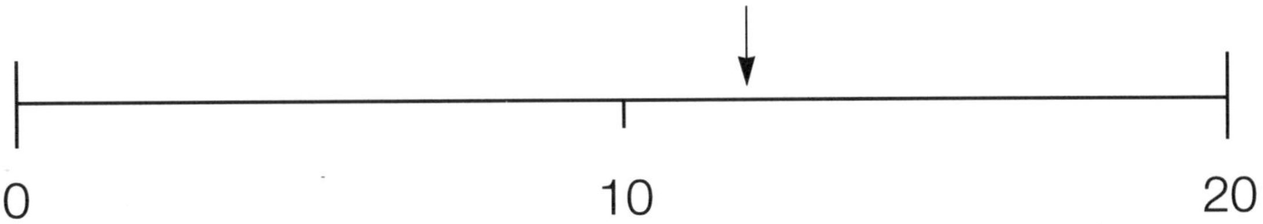

______

b 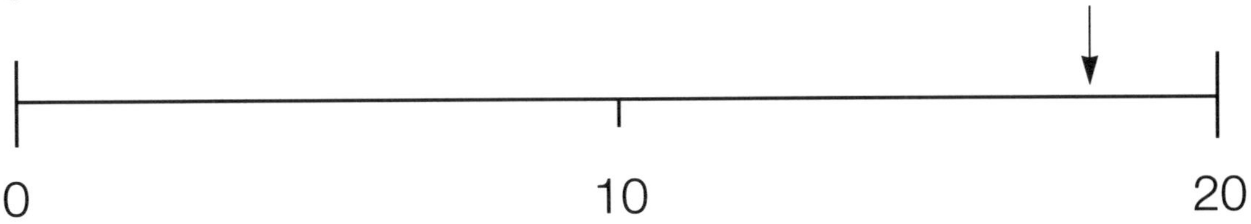

______

c 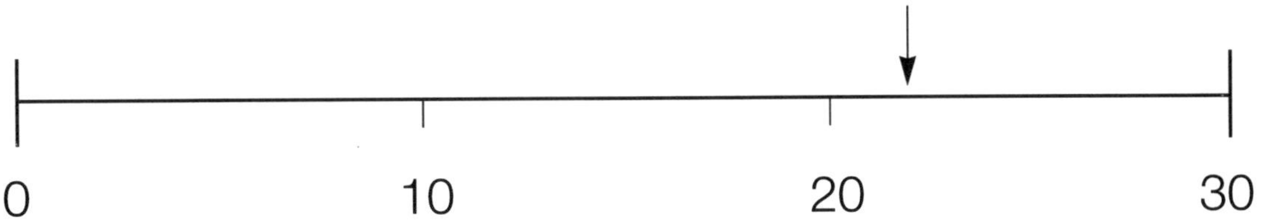

______

d 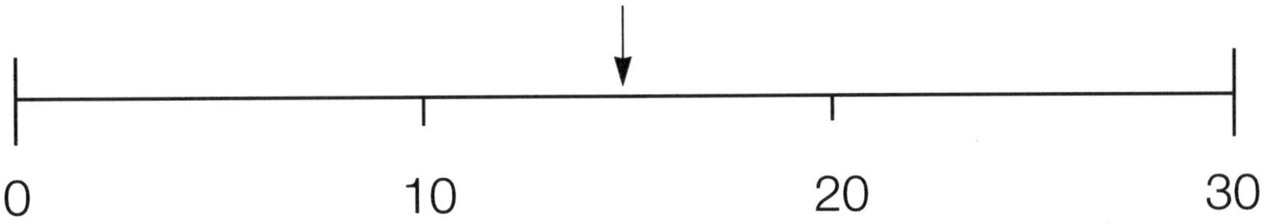

______

e 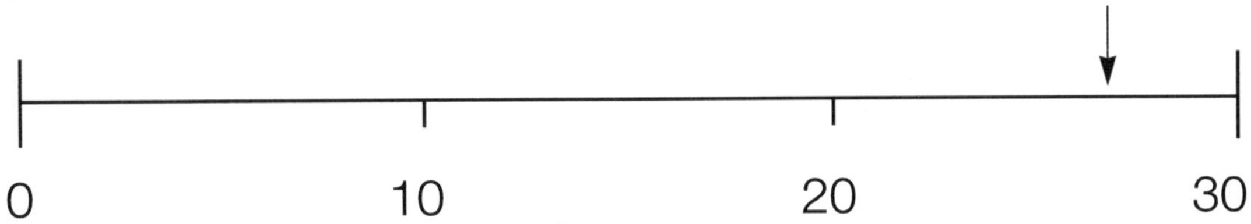

______

f 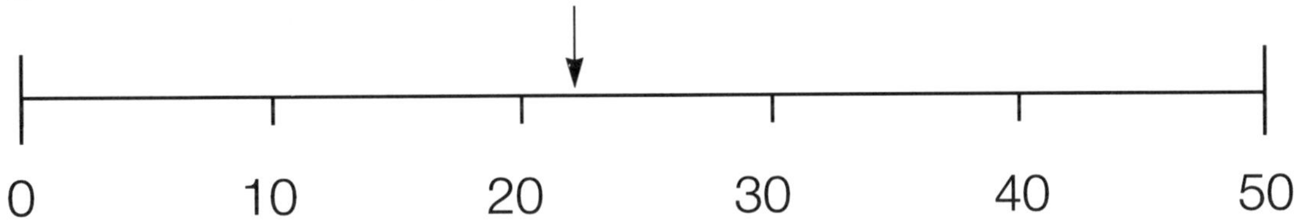

______

g 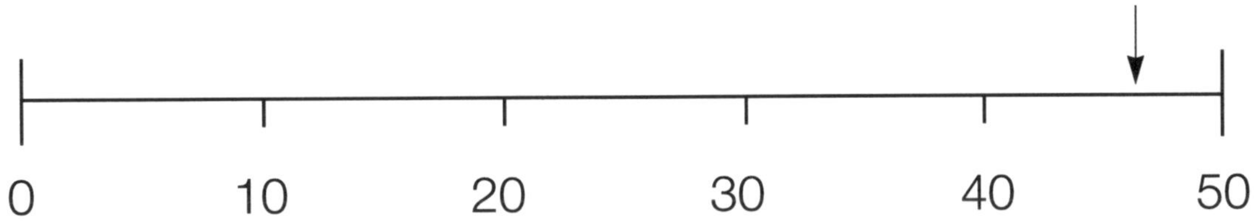

______

3. Look at this marble game. Estimate how far Tom's and Annie's marbles went.

Tom's marble went ______ cm. Annie's marble went ______ cm.

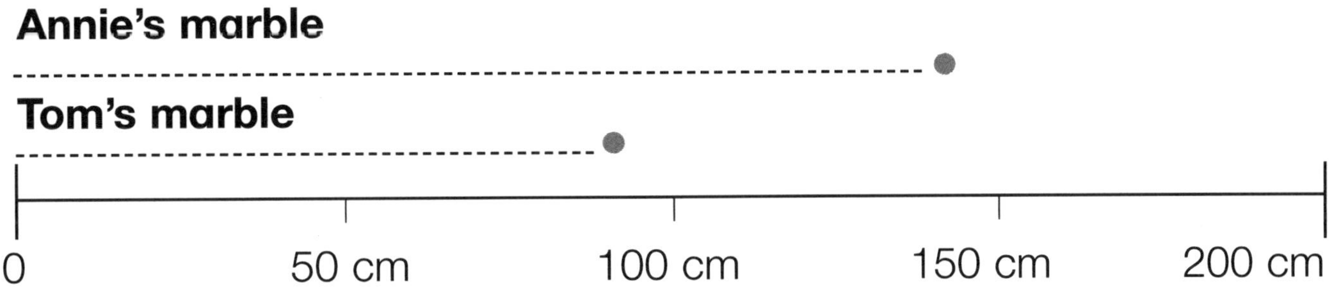

Test yourself

1. **a** 78 = ______ tens ______ units

b 32 = ______ tens ______ units

2. Which comes first?

36 or 63? ______

3. Write the number.

Six tens and eight units.

______

4. **a** 6 + 7 + 4 = ______

b 3 + 4 + 8 = ______

5. Take 7 from 20.

______

6. **a** $5 \times 10 =$ ______

b $8 \times 10 =$ ______

7. Using 2 lines cut the circle in $\frac{1}{4}$ s.

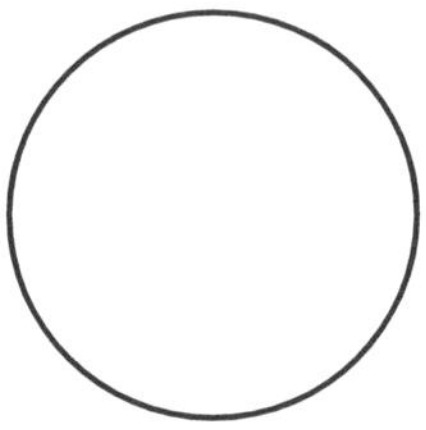

8. Odd or even?

16 = 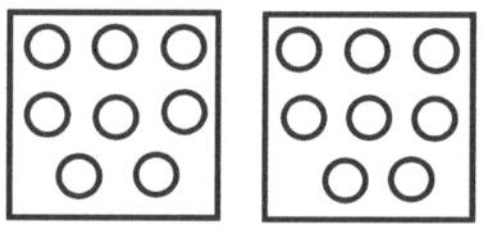 = ______

8 8

9. What is the time?

$\frac{1}{2}$ past ______

10. **a** 8 + 8 = ______

b 3 + 3 = ______

11. Fill in the gap.

12 − ______ = 7

12. What is 10 less than 65?

______

13. a $6 \times 2 =$ ______

b $10 \times 2 =$ ______

14. $9 \div 3 =$ ______

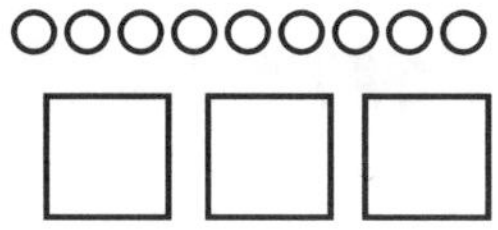

15. Measure this pencil.

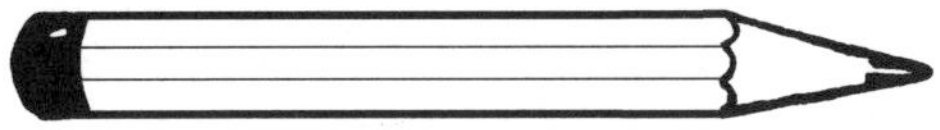

______ cm

16. Draw a straight line with a ruler. Measure it.

______ cm

17. Cut this square in $\frac{1}{3}$s.

18. Which is more?

a 68 or 72 ______

b 54 or 45 ______

19. a ______ $+ 6 = 20$

b ______ $+ 12 = 20$

20. a $5 \times 5 =$ ______

b $7 \times 5 =$ ______

21. $7 \div 2 =$ 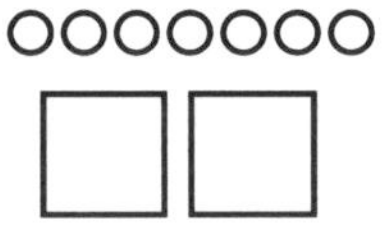 ___r___

22. The nearest ten to 18 is ______ .

23. Which numbers come next?

3 6 9 ______ **15** ______ ______

24. How many $\frac{1}{4}$s = 1 whole circle?

______ $\frac{1}{4}$s.

25. Estimate the number. ______

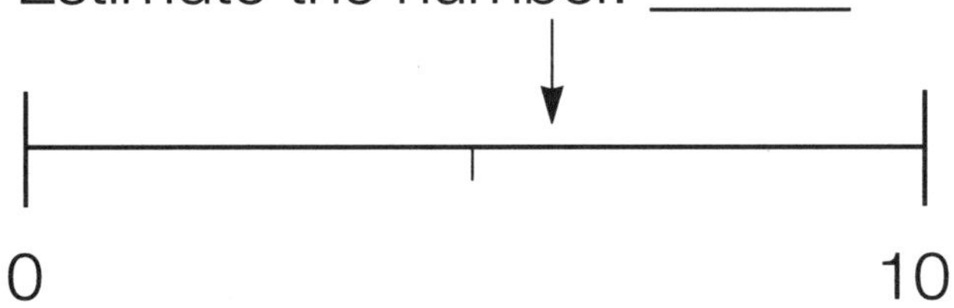

26. $3 \times 2 = 6$

$6 \div 3 =$ ______

Answers

pages 4–5

1. 9
2.  3 sides
3. a

✓	✗	✓	✗	✓	✗	✓	✗	✓

b

○	●	●	○	●	●	○	●	●

c

B	B	A	A	B	B	A	A	B

4. **a** 5 **b** 8 **c** 8
5. **a** 4 **b** 2 **c** 3
6. 
7. **a** – **b** + **c** +
8. **a** 3 6 9 **b** 2 4 6 8 10
9. **a** 16 = 1 ten 6 units **b** 11 = 1 ten 1 unit
10. 7 o'clock
11. train, ship
12. 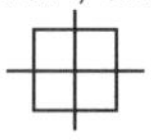

pages 6–7

1. **b** 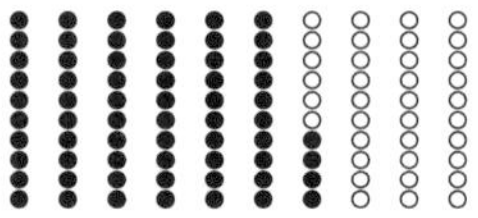 (64) **c** 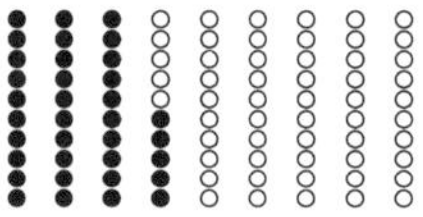 (35)
2. **a** 72 **b** 45 **c** 58
3. **a** 5 tens 3 units **b** 2 tens 8 units **c** 9 tens 7 units
   d 3 tens 6 units
4. **a** 53 **b** 35 **c** 21

pages 8–9

1. **a** 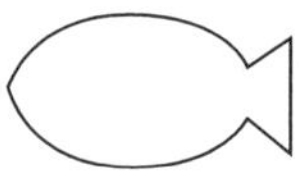 **b**  **c**  **d** 
2. **a** 64 **b** 48 **c** 87 **d** 19, 21 **e** 29, 31
3. **a** 45 **b** 21 **c** 73 **d** 11 **e** 29 **f** 46 **g** 18 **h** 12 **i** 55 **j** 69
   k 17 **l** 51
4. **a** 24 **b** 39 or 40 **c** 20 or 21 or 22 or 23 **d** 30 or 31 or 32
   e 32 **f** 69 or 70 or 71 **g** 98 **h** 69 or 70 or 71 or 72

pages 10–11

1. **a** 6 tens 3 units **b** 2 tens 8 units **c** 3 tens 5 units
   d 7 tens 6 units
2. **a** 2 tens 3 units **b** 4 tens 8 units **c** 5 tens 7 units
   d 8 tens 9 units **e** 6 tens 2 units **f** 9 tens 9 units
   g 7 tens 3 units
3. **a** four tens seven units **b** two tens nine units **c** six tens nine units
   d seven tens two units
4. **a** 65 **b** 93 **c** 22 **d** 59

pages 12–13

1. **a** 10 **b** 12 **c** 11 **d** 16
2. **a** 4 + 3 + 3 = 10 **b** 6 + 4 + 5 = 15 **c** 5 + 3 + 6 = 14
3. **a** 15 **b** 19 **c** 20 **d** 18
4. **a** 16 **b** 16 **c** *various possibilities* **d** 16 **e** *various possibilities*

pages 14–15

1. **a** 8 – 3 = 5 **b** 4 – 3 = 1 **c** 6 – 4 = 2
2. **a** 13 – 6 = 7 **b** 11 – 7 = 4 **c** 17 – 6 = 11 **d** 13 – 8 = 5
3. **a** 7 **b** 10 **c** 12 **d** 7
4. **a** 1 **b** 10 **c** 8

pages 16–17

1. **a** 50 **b** 30 **c** 70 **d** 40 **e** 10
2. 10, 20, 30, 40, 50, 60, 70, 80, 90, 100
3. **a** 60 **b** 80 **c** 3 **d** 5 **e** 10 **f** 10
4.

10	20	30	40	50	60	70	80	90

10	20	30	40	50	60	70	80	90

pages 18–19

1. 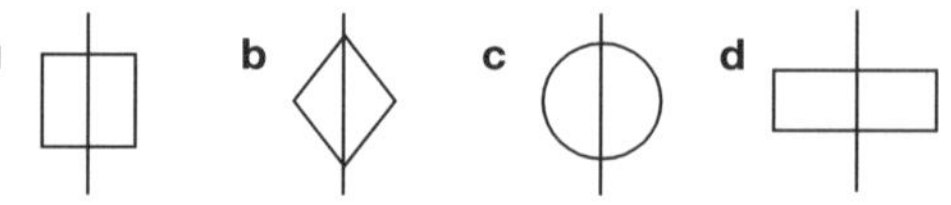

2. 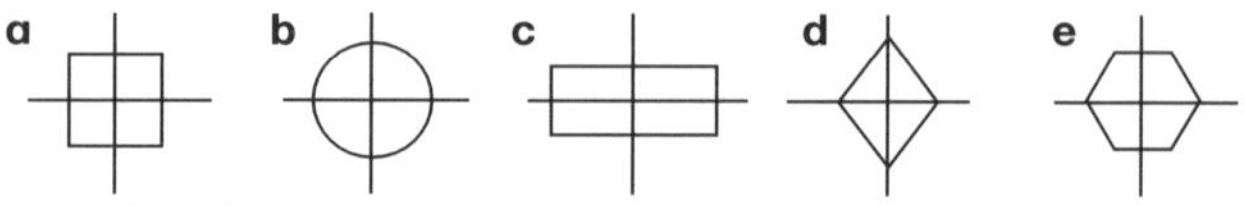

3. $\frac{1}{4}$ $\frac{1}{2}$ $\frac{1}{4}$ $\frac{1}{2}$

pages 20–21

1. **a** even **b** odd **c** odd
2. **a** 7 8 = odd **b** 4 4 = even **c** 9 10 = odd
   d 6 7 = odd **e** 9 9 = even
3.

1	2	3	4	5	6	7	8	9	10	11	12	13	14	15	16	17	18	19	20

(shaded = odd, white = even)

pages 22–23

1. **a** 6 tens and 7 units **b** 2 tens and 9 units
   c 3 tens and 6 units **d** 4 tens and 2 units
2. **a** 31, 34 **b** 73, 75 **c** 59, 62
3. **a** 33 **b** 87 **c** 65
4. **a** 15 **b** 17 **c** *various possibilities* **d** *various possibilities*
5. **a** 11 – 4 = 7 **b** 15 – 6 = 9
6. **a** 20 **b** 70 **c** 30 **d** 80
7. 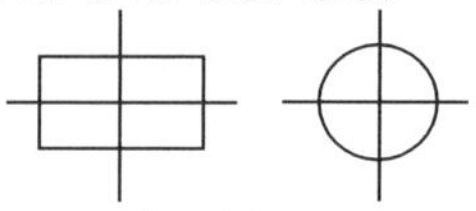
8. **a** even **b** odd

pages 24–25

1. **a** 8 o'clock **b** 3 o'clock **c** 11 o'clock
2. **a** $\frac{1}{2}$ past 10 **b** $\frac{1}{2}$ past 7 **c** $\frac{1}{2}$ past 1
3. 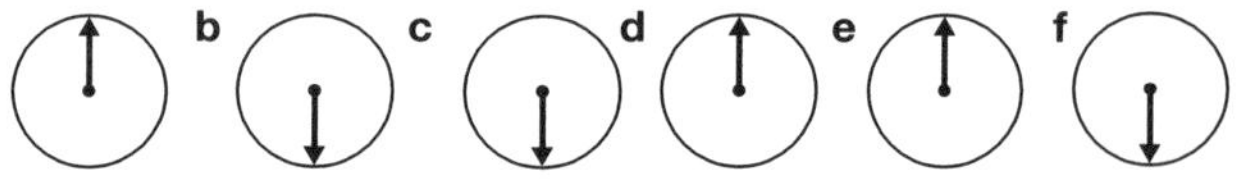

4. **a** $\frac{1}{2}$ past 7 **b** 6 o'clock
5. **a** 4 o'clock **b** $\frac{1}{2}$ past 3 **c** $\frac{1}{2}$ past 4

pages 26–27

1. 1 + 1 = 2 2 + 2 = 4 3 + 3 = 6 4 + 4 = 8 5 + 5 = 10
   6 + 6 = 12 7 + 7 = 14 8 + 8 = 16 9 + 9 = 18
   10 + 10 = 20
2. **a** 16 **b** 4 **c** 2 **d** 12 **e** 10 **f** 18 **g** 20 **h** 14
3. **a** 10 **b** 14 **c** 6
4. **a** 16p **b** 8p **c** 10p **d** 20p **e** 36p

pages 28–29

1. **a** 14 **b** 3 **c** 10 **d** 9 **e** 4 **f** 9 **g** 5 **h** 8
2. **a** 3 **b** 10 **c** 7 **d** 6 **e** 20 **f** 15 **g** 6 **h** 3
3. **a** 4 **b** 6 **c** 6 **d** 7 **e** 10 **f** 3 **g** 4
4. 13, 1

pages 30–31

1. **a** 73 **b** 80 **c** 66 **d** 82
2. **a** 17 **b** 88 **c** 24 **d** 98
3. **a** 43 **b** 51 **c** 35
4. **a** 52 **b** 36 **c** 75
5. **a**

3	13	23	33	43	53	63	73	83

b

96	86	76	66	56	46	36	26	16